Heard What's Cookin'?

A Collection of
Tantalizin' Texas Treats

Heard Museum Volunteer Guild
McKinney, Texas

Heard What's Cookin'? is a treasury of favorite recipes from members of the Heard Museum Volunteer Guild, their families and friends. Over 800 recipes were submitted and guild members tested each recipe for excellence in taste and for accuracy. Only the very best were selected for publication. We consider these recipes special, but do not claim that they are original. Brand names have been used only when considered necessary for the success of the recipe.

All proceeds raised from the sale of ***Heard What's Cookin'?*** directly benefit The Heard Natural Science Museum & Wildlife Sanctuary in its commitment to preserve, create and expand a healthy environment through education.

By
Heard Museum Volunteer Guild

Additional copies of ***Heard What's Cookin'?*** may be obtained at the cost of $16.95, plus $3.00 postage and handling, each book. Texas residents add $1.39 sales tax, each book.

Send to:

Heard Museum Volunteer Guild
One Nature Place
McKinney, TX 75069-8840

1st printing January, 1997

MISS BESSIE HEARD

The Heard Natural Science Museum & Wildlife Sanctuary owes its existence to the energy and enthusiasm of one of McKinney's leading philanthropists — Miss Bessie Heard.

During her lifetime, Miss Bessie surrounded herself with her passions — a love of nature and children. From hosting birdhouse building competitions on her front yard and planting trees to donating the land for what has become the Heard Museum, Miss Bessie committed herself to educating our city's youngsters.

Born in McKinney, TX, in 1886, Bessie was the eldest of five daughters born to John Spencer Heard and Rachel Caroline Wilson Heard. As a child, she lived a refined, cultured life that revolved around family and a love of nature.

By the turn–of–the–century standards, Miss Bessie was an unconventional woman. After attending McKinney Collegiate Institute, Bessie headed east to Virginia. She attended Mary Baldwin College for three years, where she was a member of the 1902–03 Black Diamond women's basketball team. She then traveled through Europe and Canada before enrolling in Parson's School of Design in New York City to study interior design.

Back in Texas as a young adult, Miss Bessie became one of the state's first interior decorators. She never married, though she had a very active social calendar.

Most importantly, though, Bessie Heard was an environmentalist and a passionate collector. As a young woman, she strolled the beaches of Padre Island, collecting the most beautiful sea shells she could find. During her world travels, her collections grew to include butterflies and original prints by Audubon and Redoute.

Eventually her collections, which she delighted in sharing with local children, became too large for her McKinney home. And, like her collections, McKinney was also expanding. With an eye to the future, Miss Bessie began developing a plan to establish a museum for her collections —

as well as a place of preservation and learning for the families of her burgeoning home town.

At an age when most people would consider retiring, this civic-minded doyenne consulted John Ripley Forbes, president of the National Science for Youth Foundation and began laying the ground-work for what would become her greatest civic contribution.

At the age of 80, she formed the Bessie Heard Foundation. Two years later, in 1966, construction began on the Heard Museum. Miss Bessie remained active in the project — choosing the property, overseeing construction, consulting with the director and staff. In 1967, the doors opened and Miss Bessie's dream became a reality.

This remarkable woman remained involved with the museum for the rest of her life, watching proudly as the facility bearing her name became one of the top attractions in the County.

Bessie Heard died on March 22, 1988, just two months short of her 102nd birthday. Her spirit, however, continues for all of us to enjoy.

THE HEARD NATURAL SCIENCE MUSEUM & WILDLIFE SANCTUARY

Imagine sitting on the side of a hill, rapt in the glory of a new dawn as it glides across the Texas plains. The morning breeze kisses your face. Native flowers gently nod their colorful caps, waving languidly to each other. Below, slider turtles crack the glassy surface of a tranquil pond, pushing aside reeds as they slice the water. A red-tailed hawk spreads its wings and floats overhead.

Thanks to the foresight and generosity of McKinney philanthropist Bessie Heard, this vision is a reality for all who visit the Heard Natural Science Museum & Wildlife Sanctuary. The McKinney treasure is a secluded spot dedicated to Mother Nature's bounty and the education and enjoyment of all who visit.

Built by the Bessie Heard Foundation in 1966, the museum sits on land originally operated as a dairy farm by the late Dr. Jack F. Perkins. Dr. Perkins, a personal friend of Miss Bessie, often invited her to visit his property. She did, falling in love with the beauty of the rolling prairie and tree–studded woods. When it came time to choose a site for her museum, no other piece of property would do.

Born with the mission to "Create, preserve and utilize a healthy environment while teaching visitors to understand and appreciate their surroundings," the Heard Museum opened its doors on October 1, 1967. Today, the museum has evolved into Collin County's number one cultural attraction, drawing almost 100,000 people annually.

The 274–acre wildlife sanctuary shelters more than 240 species of birds, mammals, reptiles and amphibians, as well as 150 species of wildflowers and plants. A native plant demonstration garden greets guests as they enter the museum. This two–acre outdoor classroom contains more than 135 species of native plants.

The Heard Museum also boasts a 50–acre wetland area featuring an outdoor learning center with observation deck, floating study, laboratory and boardwalk. Within the preserve, visitors can enjoy woods, prairies, creeks, ponds, hilltops, wetlands and bottom lands. The Raptor Rehabilitation Centre at the Heard is world–renowned for its work with injured or orphaned birds of prey.

Miss Bessie believed in teaching children the joys of nature. The museum bearing her name follows the same philosophy. The museum's heart lies in its extensive educational program. The staff strives to familiarize children with the characteristics of plants, animals and insects and their relationship to each other.

Each year, the museum hosts more than 5,700 children in preschool, weekend and summer activities. More than 10,000 school children come for field trip programs while more than 32,000 children from the surrounding eight–county area enjoy Heard–sponsored programs presented in their school.

The Heard Museum is located at One Nature Place on the south side of McKinney. To reach the museum, take Exit 38E from US 75. For more information, call (972) 562–5566.

COOKBOOK COMMITTEE

Gayle Brown, Chair
Sybil Carter
Valeta Cope
Ann Day
Connie Eaker
Martha Francis
Katie Johnson
Etta Mae Martin
Joan Mayo
Diane Norman
Marlys Norton
Shirley Presson
Susan Raymer
Carol Turner

Cookbook title – Teri Franzmeier
Original cover concept – Guild members
Cover concept drawing – Zachary Johnson
Cookbook artist – Bob Haydon
Museum sketch artist – Georgia Curry
Miss Bessie Heard and Heard Museum narratives – Julie Vargo
Organization page – Shirley Presson

RECIPE CONTRIBUTORS

Norma Allen
Jack Allen
Susan Barkley
Denise Billings
Pat Bird
Lavauda Branch
Gayle Brown
Constance Caldwell
Sybil Carter
Joan Celeste
Ellen Colaninni
Ruth Cooper
Valeta Cope
Eunice Cox
Mary Will Craig
Gera Crampton
Janebell Crowe
Georgia Curry
Ann Day
Richard Dill
Lorre Dratch
Jan Drummond
Connie Eaker
Sharon Eatherly
Kathryn Eubanks
Martha N. Francis
Martha V. Francis
Teri Franzmeier
Billie Gage
Alane Porter Griggs
Arline Grindle
Peggy Guarnacci
Phyllis Gulotta
Geri Haas
Edith A. Hogan
Joyce Holland
Mary Honeycutt
Sue Horn
Sylvia Jabara
Katie Johnson
Barbara Luckiesh
Etta Mae Martin
Joan Mayo
Stacey Tainter McIntyre
Karen McPeek
Marci Meyer
Joyce Moneta
Lynda Moneta
Dorothy E. Moore
Loes Munster
Clema Myrick
Diane Norman
Marlys Norton
Rhonda Olson
Maxine Ousley
Gerry Palmer
Ester M. Peck
Clara Mae Perkins
Klema Perry
Mary Porter
Mike Porter
Reid Presson
Shirley Presson
Susan Raymer
Elizabeth Bush Roberts
Debbie Sedgwick
Fran Smith
Maria Smith
Marcella Sokol
Virginia Sorensen
Mary Doris Sutherland
Ruby Swanner
Betty Tafel
Elaine Thomson
Carol Turner
Dolores Ueckert
Donna Westdyke
Sue Williams
Rosemary Wisniewsky
Ella Weeter

TABLE OF CONTENTS

THE HEARD MUSEUM VOLUNTEER GUILD

The result of the benevolence of Miss Bessie Heard through the Bessie Heard Foundation, the Heard Natural Science Museum & Wildlife Sanctuary became a reality in 1967.

Recognizing the need for volunteers to further the work begun by Miss Bess, the Heard Museum Volunteer Guild was organized in 1969 with nine charter members. This fledgling group had big dreams and a strong resolve. The guild adopted a statement of purpose "to stimulate public interest in the Heard Natural Science Museum & Wildlife Sanctuary and to assist and participate in the museum's activities."

Today, with a growing and vibrant membership exceeding 100, the purpose of the guild remains the same; however, fund–raising has become an important part of the guild's activities. The guild hosts four fund–raising events annually — food service for Family Fun Festival in September; Fall Review and luncheon in October; Game Day at the Heard and luncheon in January; and Spring Fashion Show and luncheon in March. Each has become a widely accepted and highly anticipated event.

The guild's catering committee prepares and serves all the food for the luncheons and special events, as well as catering private and business luncheons, by reservation, at the museum. The guild's reputation is solid as an organization of great cooks. ***Heard What's Cookin'?*** is a collection of the "best of the best" recipes from our great cooks.

Through the years, common interests have enriched the lives of the members of the Heard Museum Volunteer Guild. Some people have dreams, some have fantasies, and others have visions. Surely, the nine charter members of the guild were visionaries who created an organization of which to be proud. There is a feeling that somewhere Miss Bess has a smile of satisfaction on her face for "a job well done!"

The Heard Natural Science Museum & Wildlife Sanctuary is a non-profit organization serving eight counties with educational programs for school children. All proceeds raised by the Volunteer Guild benefit the museum in its ever expanding outreach to the community.

Appetizers & Beverages

CRABMEAT SPREAD

- **2 7-ounce cans drained crabmeat**
- **½ cup mayonnaise**
- **2 teaspoons horseradish**
- **2 tablespoons lemon juice**
- **2 tablespoons minced green onion**
- **1 teaspoon salt**
- **¼ teaspoon pepper**
- **paprika**

Combine all ingredients except paprika. Cover and chill. Sprinkle with paprika before serving with crackers.

Yield: 2 cups

BILLIE JEAN'S SHRIMP DIP

- **2 cups cooked popcorn shrimp**
- **1 8-ounce package softened cream cheese**
- **5 chopped green onions**
- **1 teaspoon Worcestershire sauce**
- **3 small shakes Tabasco sauce**
- **juice of 1 lemon**
- **mayonnaise for consistency**
- **seasoned salt to taste**

Mix all ingredients together and chill. Serve with crackers.

Yield: 3 cups

EASY SHRIMP DIP

- **1 7-ounce can tiny cooked shrimp**
- **1 0.7-ounce package dry zesty Italian dressing**
- **1 8-ounce package cream cheese**
- **1 8-ounce container sour cream**

Mix all ingredients together and serve with crackers.

Yield: 2 cups

SALMON DIP

- **1 6½-ounce can drained salmon**
- **1 12-ounce container softened fat free cream cheese**
- **¼ cup finely chopped green onions including some green tops**
- **1 tablespoon finely chopped red bell pepper**

Place salmon, cream cheese and 3 tablespoons green onions in mixing bowl. Mix well with fork until smooth. Garnish with red bell pepper and remaining tablespoon of green onions. Chill until serving time.

Yield: 2 cups

SOUTHWEST SEVEN LAYER DIP

In a 9x13 inch glass dish, layer in the following order:

LAYER #1:

Mix together:

- **3 large mashed avocados**
- **⅛ teaspoon garlic powder**
- **⅛ teaspoon garlic salt**
- **1 tablespoon lemon juice**
- **2 tablespoons mayonnaise**

LAYER #2:

- **1 8-ounce container sour cream**

LAYER #3:

- **½-1 cup medium picante sauce**

LAYER #4:

- **¾ cup chopped ripe olives**

LAYER #5:

- **3 cups fresh chopped tomatoes (approximately 3 medium)**

LAYER #6:

- **6 chopped green onions with tops**

LAYER #7:

- **1½ cups grated Cheddar cheese**

Best if prepared 1 to 2 hours before serving. Serve with corn chips as a dip. Can also be used as a salad with Mexican food.

Yield: 20 servings

Bats are the only mammals that fly.

PIÑA COLADA DIP

1 8-ounce package cream cheese
¼ cup sugar
2 tablespoons milk
2 9⁄16-ounce packages piña colada mix
2 tablespoons rum

Soften cream cheese and mix with remaining ingredients. Serve with fresh fruit slices.

Yield: 8-10 servings

EASY GARLIC CHEESE ROLL

1 16-ounce package grated Cheddar cheese
2 8-ounce packages cream cheese
2 processed garlic cloves
chili powder

Combine all ingredients and mix well. Shape into log or roll. Roll in chili powder. Chill and slice. Serve on crackers.

Yield: 6-8 servings

TEXAS PECAN CHEESE BALL

2 8-ounce packages softened cream cheese
1 8-ounce can drained crushed pineapple
2 tablespoons dried minced onions
1 finely chopped green pepper
1 cup chopped pecans
salt to taste

Mix together all ingredients except nuts. Shape into ball or log and roll in nuts. Refrigerate several hours before serving. Serve with crackers or bagel chips.

Yield: 6-8 servings

BITE SIZE CHEESE BALLS

1 3-ounce package cream cheese
1 cup finely shredded Cheddar cheese
¾ cup finely shredded carrots
1 tablespoon honey
½ cup finely chopped pecans
24 pretzel sticks (small)

Combine first 4 ingredients; cover and chill 1 hour. Shape into 1 inch balls and roll in pecans; cover and chill. To serve, place a pretzel in each.

Yield: 24 pieces

GINGER CHEESE

1 8-ounce package softened cream cheese
2 tablespoons half and half
3 tablespoons chopped crystallized ginger
2 tablespoons toasted almond slices
ginger snaps

Combine cream cheese and half and half. Beat at medium speed with electric mixer until smooth. Stir in ginger and chill for 8 hours. Sprinkle with almonds and serve with ginger snaps.

Yield: 1 cup

DEVILED HAM AND CHEESE SPREAD

1 2¼-ounce can deviled ham
1 3-ounce package softened cream cheese
½ teaspoon lemon juice
½ teaspoon horseradish

Combine all ingredients. Serve with crackers.

Yield: ¾ cup

HAM AND MELON KABOBS WITH MUSTARD SAUCE

- 1 1-inch thick slice cubed cooked ham
- 1 cantaloupe
- 1 honeydew melon
- ¼ cup sugar
- 2 teaspoons mustard
- 2 teaspoons vegetable oil
- ½ cup salad dressing
- ½ teaspoon garlic powder

Cut cantaloupe and melon into chunks. Alternate chunks of ham, cantaloupe, and honeydew melon on small bamboo skewers or large ones that have been cut in half. Mix together sugar, mustard and vegetable oil and add the salad dressing and garlic powder. Drizzle the sauce over the kabobs.

Yield: 8 large skewers or 16 small skewers

TORTILLA SWIRLS

- 1 8-ounce package fat free cream cheese
- 1 cup shredded Monterey Jack cheese
- 2 tablespoons dried minced onions
- ½ teaspoon seasoned salt
- ⅛ teaspoon garlic powder
- 2 15-ounce cans drained black beans
- 8 6 inch flour tortillas
- salsa

Mix together first 5 ingredients and refrigerate for 2 hours. Process black beans in blender until smooth, or mash with fork, or chop very fine. Spread thin layer of black beans on each tortilla. Top with thin layer of cream cheese mixture. Roll up tightly and wrap in plastic wrap. Refrigerate 4 or 5 hours or until set. Slice and dip into salsa. Freezes well.

Yield: 16-20 servings

BLACK BEAN SALSA

- 1 15-ounce can black beans
- 1 12-ounce jar hot, medium, or mild salsa
- ¼ cup chopped fresh cilantro
- ¼ teaspoon cumin
- 2 tablespoons freshly squeezed lime juice

Chop beans; stir in salsa, cilantro, cumin, and lime juice. Refrigerate or serve immediately. Serve with chips or sliced vegetables.

Yield: 3 cups

TEXAS TORTILLAS

- **1 8-ounce package cream cheese**
- **1 8-ounce container sour cream**
- **1 cup shredded Cheddar cheese**
- **⅓ cup chopped onion**
- **1 4-ounce can chopped black olives**
- **garlic salt**
- **1 4-ounce can chopped chilies**
- **4 10 inch flour tortillas**
- **salsa**

Blend all ingredients, except tortillas and salsa. Spread mixture on tortillas. Roll and wrap in plastic wrap. Chill several hours. Slice approximately ⅜-inch thick and serve with salsa.

Yield: 16-20 servings

 *Some bats beat their wings as many as 20 times per second.*

SPICY SHRIMP

- **1¾ pounds large raw shrimp**
- **2 tablespoons sweet butter**
- **1 tablespoon olive oil**
- **1 tablespoon finely minced garlic**
- **2 tablespoons finely minced shallots**
- **salt and freshly ground pepper to taste**
- **2 tablespoons lemon juice, or to taste**
- **2 tablespoons finely chopped fresh dill**

Peel and devein shrimp. In a large skillet, over low heat, melt butter with olive oil. Add garlic and shallots, sauté for 2 minutes without browning. Add shrimp, increase heat slightly, and cook 3 minutes or until done to taste. Add salt and pepper to taste and toss well. Remove to a bowl, scraping in all the sauce. Add lemon juice and dill; toss together well. Cover and refrigerate 3 to 4 hours before serving. Serve as a first course or on the ends of long bamboo skewers as an appetizer.

Yield: 10 hors d'oeuvre servings or 4-6 appetizer servings

ICED CAULIFLOWER

1 large head cauliflower
1 8-ounce bottle Italian dressing
1 cup frozen prepared guacamole

Cook or steam whole cauliflower until tender-crisp. Marinate overnight in Italian dressing. Remove from dressing and ice with guacamole. Serve with buttery crackers.

Yield: 20 servings

BROCCOLI DIP

2 10-ounce packages frozen chopped broccoli
1 cup butter or margarine
1 large chopped onion
2 10¾-ounce cans cream of mushroom soup
2 6-ounce rolls diced garlic cheese
salt and pepper to taste
1 8-ounce can drained, chopped mushroom pieces
½ cup slivered almonds (optional)

Cook broccoli according to directions and drain. Sauté onions in butter and add all ingredients except mushrooms and almonds. Simmer until cheese is melted. Add mushrooms and sprinkle almonds on top, if desired. Serve in chafing dish with large size corn chips.

Yield: 12 servings

THE BEST HOT CRAB DIP

2 8-ounce packages cubed cream cheese
2 6½-ounce cans drained crabmeat
1 minced garlic clove
½ cup mayonnaise
2 teaspoons prepared mustard
¼ cup sherry
1 tablespoon minced onion
seasoned salt to taste

Combine cheese, crabmeat, garlic, mayonnaise, mustard, sherry and onion in a heavy saucepan. Heat until cheese is melted and sauce is smooth, stirring occasionally. Season to taste with seasoned salt. Transfer to a chafing dish and serve with an assortment of crackers.

Yield: 3 cups

BLACK BEAN DIP

- **1 15-ounce can drained black beans**
- **1 8-ounce can tomato sauce**
- **½ cup shredded Cheddar cheese**
- **1 teaspoon chili powder**
- **additional shredded Cheddar cheese (optional)**

Combine beans and tomato sauce in a small saucepan; bring to a boil over medium heat, stirring occasionally. Remove from heat. Mash beans with a potato masher or with the back of a spoon. Add ½ cup Cheddar cheese and chili powder; cook, stirring constantly, until cheese melts. Garnish with additional shredded cheese. Serve dip warm with chips or assorted vegetables.

Yield: 2 cups

CORN DIP

- **½ cup butter**
- **1 8-ounce package cream cheese**
- **1 16-ounce can whole kernel corn**
- **1-3 tablespoons finely chopped pickled jalapeño peppers**
- **cumin to taste**

Melt butter in microwave. Add cream cheese and whisk until smooth. Drain corn and reserve juice. Add corn, peppers and cumin to taste. If dip is too thick, add some of the juice. Serve warm in chafing dish with corn chips. If mixture separates, whisk again.

Yield: 3 cups

Note: May use low fat or fat free cream cheese.

GREEN CHILI PIE

- **2 4-ounce cans drained, chopped green chilies**
- **4 well beaten eggs**
- **1 10-ounce package shredded Cheddar cheese**
- **2 tablespoons sour cream**

Lightly grease a 9 inch pie pan with butter. Spread chilies evenly on bottom of pan and add cheese. Drizzle beaten eggs over cheese. Top with sour cream. Bake at 325 degrees for 30-35 minutes until set. Cut into bite size pieces.

Yield: 12 servings

TEXAS TORTE

- 2 beaten eggs
- 2 tablespoons all purpose flour
- ½ teaspoon salt
- ⅓ cup milk
- 1 4-ounce can mild green chilies
- ½ pound grated sharp Cheddar cheese
- ½ pound grated Monterey Jack cheese

Add flour, salt and milk to beaten eggs. Beat well. Add remaining ingredients and mix well. Pour into flat, well-greased 8x12 inch glass baking dish. Bake at 350 degrees for 35 minutes. Cut into squares and serve hot. Freezes well.

Yield: 15 servings

ARTICHOKE CHEESE SQUARES

- ⅓ cup chopped onion
- 1 mashed garlic clove (optional)
- 2 tablespoons bacon fat
- 4 beaten eggs
- 1 14-ounce can drained, chopped artichoke hearts
- ¼ cup dry bread crumbs
- ½ pound shredded Swiss cheese
- 2 tablespoons minced parsley
- ¼ teaspoon oregano
- ⅛ teaspoon Tabasco sauce
- ½ teaspoon salt
- pepper to taste

Sauté onion and garlic in fat. Beat eggs until frothy, and combine with remaining ingredients. Bake in a greased 7x11 inch baking dish at 325 degrees for 25 to 30 minutes. Cut into 1½ inch squares to serve.

Yield: 12 servings

BUFFALO WINGS

- ¼ cup dry sherry
- ¼ teaspoon garlic powder
- ¼ teaspoon pepper
- ½ cup soy sauce
- ¼ cup cider vinegar
- ½ teaspoon salt
- ½ cup honey
- 2-3 pounds chicken wings or legettes

Mix all ingredients and pour over chicken. Marinate overnight or at least 3 hours. Bake in a single layer for 1 hour, 15 minutes at 325 degrees. Pour off most of sauce after 45 minutes and continue baking until brown.

Yield: 24-36 servings

GOLDEN CHICKEN TRIANGLES

6 ounces softened cream cheese
6 tablespoons melted margarine
4 cups cooked, cubed chicken breast
½ teaspoon salt
¼ teaspoon pepper
4 tablespoons milk
2 tablespoons chopped chives
2 tablespoons chopped pimento
2 8-ounce cans refrigerated quick crescent dinner rolls
1½ cups seasoned crouton crumbs

Heat oven to 350 degrees. In a bowl, blend cheese and 4 tablespoons margarine until smooth. Add next 6 ingredients and mix well. Separate crescent dough into 8 rectangles. Firmly press perforations to seal. Spoon ½ cup meat mixture onto center of each rectangle. Put 4 corners to top of chicken mixture and twist slightly. Seal edges. Brush tops with 2 tablespoons melted margarine. Dip in crouton crumbs. Place on ungreased cookie sheet. Bake at 350 degrees for 20-25 minutes until golden brown.

Yield: 8 rectangles; if cut in thirds, makes 24 appetizer portions

ROLL UPS LA COSTA

8-10 ounces softened cream cheese
1½ teaspoons garlic salt
2-3 tablespoons bacon bits
1 loaf light wheat bread
1 15-ounce can tall asparagus
¾ cup melted margarine or butter
Parmesan cheese on top

Mix first 3 ingredients. Roll out bread with rolling pin to make thinner. Put cheese mixture on top of bread and spread. Put 1 piece of asparagus diagonally on top of mixture and roll up. You may need a toothpick to keep together; roll each one in melted butter and sprinkle Parmesan cheese on top. Place on cookie sheet. Cook at 350 degrees for 20 to 25 minutes, turning half way through. Remove from pan and cut in half, if desired. Serve hot.

Yield: 20, or 40 if cut in half

Note: Crusts may be removed or left on - delicious either way.

PECAN BEEF DELIGHT

- 2 3-ounce packages softened low fat cream cheese
- 1 16-ounce container low fat sour cream
- 2 4-ounce jars chopped dried beef
- ½ cup finely chopped green pepper
- 2 tablespoons finely chopped onion
- ½ teaspoon garlic powder

TOPPING:

- ¾ cup chopped pecans
- 1 tablespoon butter

Blend cheese and sour cream until smooth. Fold in dried beef, green pepper, onion and garlic powder. Spoon into glass pie plate or quiche dish which has been lightly greased. Brown chopped pecans in butter for 3 minutes. Sprinkle pecans on top and bake at 300 degrees for 20 minutes or until bubbly. Serve with salt free wheat thins.

Yield: 20 servings

HAM CRESCENT SWIRLS

- 1 8-ounce can refrigerated crescent dinner rolls
- 4 thin slices of ham
- 4 teaspoons prepared mustard
- 1 cup shredded Swiss or Cheddar cheese
- 2 tablespoons sesame seeds

Heat oven to 375 degrees. Unroll dough into 4 long rectangles. Press perforations to seal. Place ham slices on dough. Spread with mustard and sprinkle with cheese. Starting on shortest side, roll up each rectangle. Press edges to seal. Coat rolls with sesame seeds. Cut each roll into 5 slices. Place, cut side down, on baking sheet. Bake at 375 degrees for 15 to 20 minutes or until golden brown. Remove immediately and garnish as desired. Serve warm.

Yield: 20 appetizers

 *Bats can live to be 20 years old or more.*

SWISS CRABMEAT BITES

1 8-ounce can drained, chopped water chestnuts
1 6-ounce can drained, flaked crabmeat
1 cup shredded Swiss cheese
½ cup mayonnaise
1½ tablespoons sliced green onions
½ teaspoon curry powder (optional)
1 teaspoon lemon juice
2 10-ounce packages refrigerated biscuits

Combine all ingredients except biscuits and mix well. Separate each biscuit into halves. Place on ungreased baking sheet. Spoon 1 rounded teaspoon of crabmeat mixture on each biscuit. Bake at 400 degrees for 10 to 12 minutes or until lightly browned.

Yield: 40 appetizer servings

BAKED TATER-DIPPED VEGGIES

1 cup instant potato flakes
⅓ cup grated Parmesan cheese
½ teaspoon celery salt
¼ teaspoon garlic powder
¼ cup melted and cooled butter or margarine
2 eggs
4-5 cups raw bite-size vegetables (mushrooms, peppers, broccoli, cauliflower, zucchini and/or parboiled carrots)

In a small bowl, combine potato flakes, Parmesan cheese, celery salt, garlic powder and butter. In another bowl, beat eggs. Dip vegetables, one at a time, into egg mixture, then into potato mixture; coat well. Place on an ungreased baking sheet. Bake at 400 degrees for 20-25 minutes. Serve with dressing or dip if desired.

Yield: 6-8 servings

ITALIAN STUFFED MUSHROOMS

15 large mushrooms
2 ounces finely chopped pepperoni
½ cup finely chopped red bell pepper
1 tablespoon canned diced jalapeño pepper
4 ounces shredded Monterey Jack cheese

Remove stems from mushrooms. Mix remaining ingredients. Fill mushrooms caps. Microwave 1½ to 2 minutes on high or until cheese melts.

Yield: 15 servings

DELICIOUS CHEESE FINGERS

2 loaves thin sliced bread (1 to 2 days old)
1 pound bulk Cheddar cheese
1 pound softened margarine

Trim crusts from bread slices and set aside. Finely shred cheese. Mix cheese and margarine with an electric mixer until very smooth. (It will never be totally smooth.) Spread mixture on one side of bread and stack 3 deep. Cut each stack into fingers. Ice each side, except bottom, and place on wax paper on a cookie sheet and place in freezer until cheese is hard. Store in plastic bag and bake as needed. Bake frozen at 350 degrees for 12-15 minutes.

Yield: 36-42 fingers

CHEEZY COOKIES

1 cup softened margarine
1 cup shredded sharp Cheddar cheese
2 cups all purpose flour
½ teaspoon salt
½ teaspoon cayenne pepper
1 teaspoon lemon juice

Beat margarine with electric mixer until creamy. Gradually add cheese and beat until well mixed. Combine flour, salt and cayenne pepper; add slowly to cheese mixture. Beat with mixer until well blended. Add lemon juice and beat until very fluffy, about 10 minutes. Drop by spoonful onto ungreased cookie sheet and bake at 300 degrees for 20 minutes. May also be piped through pastry bag for decorative cookie.

Yield: 6 dozen

YUM YUMS

8 ounces shredded Cheddar cheese
2 ounces chopped black olives
¼ cup chopped onions
¼-½ cup salad dressing
cocktail rye bread

Combine all ingredients except bread and put mixture on rye bread. Place on large cookie sheet or 2 small cookie sheets. Bake at 300 degrees for 15 minutes.

Yield: 25 servings

MUSHROOM CHEESE STROMBOLI

- ¼ pound sliced fresh mushrooms
- 1 tablespoon butter or margarine
- 1 pound loaf frozen bread dough
- 3 ounces thin sliced pepperoni
- 6 ounces thin sliced mozzarella cheese
- ¼ pound thinly slivered Provolone cheese
- 1 cup grated Parmesan cheese
- ⅓ cup spaghetti sauce
- 1 tablespoon parsley flakes
- ½ teaspoon dried oregano
- 1 egg yolk
- ½ teaspoon water
- Parmesan cheese for top

Sauté mushrooms in butter. Lightly flour board and roll dough into 30x8 inch rectangle. Cut into 2 pieces, each 15x8 inches. On the long side of each piece, put all ingredients except egg and water. Fold over dough and pinch to seal. Combine egg and water and brush over edges and end of dough. Place on greased cookie sheet and sprinkle with Parmesan cheese. Cut five small vents in top of each roll. Bake at 350 degrees for 20 minutes or until golden brown, cut into small pieces and serve warm.

Yield: 30

MISSISSIPPI DELTA CHEESE ROLLS

- 1 pound shredded extra sharp Cheddar cheese
- ⅓ cup mayonnaise
- 2 tablespoons milk
- 1 tablespoon dried parsley
- 6 finely chopped green onions
- 1 tablespoon Worcestershire sauce
- 1 teaspoon Tabasco sauce
- ½ teaspoon onion powder
- ½ teaspoon seasoned salt
- ½ teaspoon black pepper
- ½ teaspoon cayenne pepper
- 1 loaf sliced white bread
- ½ cup melted butter

Combine all ingredients except bread and melted butter. For each roll, remove crusts and flatten each slice of bread with a rolling pin. Spread with cheese mixture. Roll bread diagonally and secure with a toothpick. Place rolls on a cookie sheet and brush with melted butter. Bake at 375 degrees until cheese is melted and bread is golden brown, about 10-12 minutes.

Yield: 24 rolls

LIME PUNCH

- **1 46-ounce can lime citrus drink**
- **2 12-ounce cans frozen limeade concentrate**
- **¼ cup sugar**
- **¼ cup lime juice**
- **1 1-quart carton softened lime sherbet**
- **1 2-liter bottle ginger ale**
- **lime slices**

In a punch bowl, combine citrus drink, thawed limeade, sugar, lime juice and sherbet; stir until smooth and sugar is dissolved. Add ginger ale; stir to mix. Float lime slices on top of punch. Serve immediately.

Yield: 20-24 servings (l gallon)

STRAWBERRY PUNCH

- **1 3-ounce package strawberry gelatin**
- **2 cups hot water**
- **1 cup sugar**
- **1 quart water**
- **1 12-ounce can frozen concentrate lemonade**
- **1 quart apple juice**
- **2 quarts ginger ale**
- **½ gallon strawberry sherbet**
- **strawberries**

Dissolve gelatin in hot water. Stir in sugar and add remaining ingredients. Add ginger ale and sherbet just before serving. Garnish with strawberries.

Yield: 50 (4-ounce) servings

CRANBERRY DELIGHT PUNCH

- **1 3-ounce package cherry gelatin**
- **1 cup boiling water**
- **1 6-ounce can frozen pink lemonade**
- **1 quart cranberry cocktail juice**
- **2 cups water**
- **1 pint ginger ale**

Dissolve gelatin in 1 cup boiling water; stir in lemonade, cranberry juice and 2 cups of water. Add ginger ale and chill.

Yield: 25 (4-ounce) servings

GINGER FRUIT PUNCH

- **1 quart orange juice**
- **1 quart grapefruit juice**
- **1 quart pineapple juice**
- **1 cup lemon juice**
- **1 cup lime juice**
- **sugar to taste (optional)**
- **9 quarts ginger ale**
- **strawberries and pineapple tidbits to garnish (optional)**

Blend together all ingredients except ginger ale. Freeze in wide-mouth containers or plastic freezer bags. When ready to use, thaw to slush. Place in punch bowl and pour ginger ale over slush.

Yield: 100 (4-ounce) servings

Note: Add orange sherbet to sweeten or to make a richer punch.

TROPICAL PUNCH

- **6 cups water**
- **4 cups sugar**
- **1 46-ounce can pineapple juice**
- **5 large bananas (medium ripe)**
- **2 12-ounce cans frozen orange juice**
- **1 12-ounce can frozen lemonade**
- **ginger ale or champagne**
- **sliced strawberries**

Dissolve sugar in water, add thawed juices, mash and purée bananas; add to juice. Place in large-mouth containers and freeze. Remove from freezer 4 to 6 hours before serving (should be slushy). Add equal amounts of ginger ale or champagne. Float sliced strawberries on top.

Yield: 6 quarts

PLANTATION COFFEE PUNCH

- **2 ounces instant coffee**
- **2 quarts hot water**
- **2 cups sugar**
- **2 quarts half and half**
- **1 quart ginger ale**
- **1 pint whipped heavy cream**
- **½ gallon French vanilla ice cream**

Dissolve instant coffee in hot water and cool. Add sugar and half and half and mix well. Chill in refrigerator until serving time. When ready to use, add ginger ale, whipped cream and ice cream and stir to mix.

Yield: 60 (4-ounce) servings

LOW CAL SPICED TEA MIX

- 1 cup low cal lemon flavored tea mix
- 3 tablespoons sugar free Tang
- 1 tablespoon pie spice
- 1 0.23-ounce package powdered lemonade mix, sweetened with Nutrasweet

Mix together all ingredients and store in air tight container. Use 1½ teaspoons mix in a cup of boiling water.

Yield: 32 (1½-teaspoon) servings

ALMOND TEA

BASE:

- ¾ cup sugar
- 4 tablespoons instant tea
- 2 cups boiling water
- 1 12-ounce can lemonade
- 3 teaspoons almond extract
- 3 teaspoons vanilla extract

To make the base, mix together all ingredients. Store in refrigerator until needed.

To make the tea, combine 1 cup of base with 2½ cups of water. Adjust proportions to taste.

Yield: 3½ cups base

HARVARD TEA

- 1 handful of fresh mint
- 5 level tablespoons instant tea
- 2 cups boiling water
- ⅔ cup lemon juice
- 1¾ cups sugar

Pour boiling water over tea and mint. Steep 2 minutes. Pour into a 1 gallon container. Add lemon juice and sugar. Fill to top with water. Refrigerate.

Yield: 1 gallon

 *Female rabbits are typically larger than male rabbits.*

Soups & Sandwiches

REID'S SPECIAL GAZPACHO

- **1 28-ounce can chopped tomatoes**
- **1 large peeled and seeded cucumber**
- **1 medium seeded green bell pepper**
- **1 medium seeded red bell pepper**
- **¼ cup green onions**
- **2 garlic cloves**
- **⅓ cup extra-virgin olive oil**
- **3 tablespoons balsamic vinegar**
- **2 teaspoons hot pepper sauce**
- **1 teaspoon ground cumin**
- **1 11.5-ounce can tomato juice**
- **salt and pepper**

Place tomatoes in large bowl; chop vegetables and garlic into chunks; add to tomatoes.

Pour into food processor and pulse until all vegetables are finely chopped but not puréed. Return to bowl and add remaining ingredients, adjusting to taste. Refrigerate until chilled.

Yield: 6–8 servings

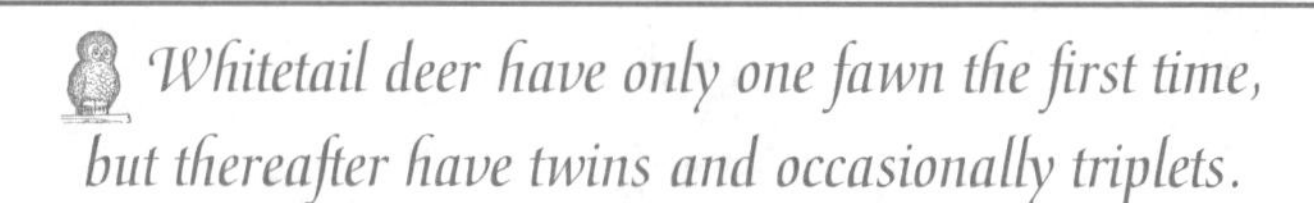

Whitetail deer have only one fawn the first time, but thereafter have twins and occasionally triplets.

CRAB BISQUE

- **1 10¾-ounce can cream of mushroom soup**
- **2 soup cans milk**
- **2½ ounces grated Swiss cheese**
- **1 14½-ounce can cream style corn**
- **2 4-ounce cans crabmeat or 8-ounces frozen crabmeat**
- **¼ teaspoons curry powder**
- **1 teaspoon salt**
- **few drops hot sauce**

Combine all ingredients except crab and bring to boil. Add crabmeat and simmer 10 minutes.

Yield: 4 servings

BACON POTATO SOUP

8 slices bacon
1 cup chopped onion
2 cups diced potatoes
1 cup water
1 teaspoon seasoned salt
⅛ teaspoon pepper
1 10¾–ounce can cream of chicken soup
1 cup sour cream
1½ cups milk

Cut bacon into ½ inch pieces. In a 3 quart saucepan, fry bacon over medium heat until browned. Add onion and continue cooking for 3 minutes or until tender. Drain; add potatoes, water, salt and pepper. Continue cooking for about 20 minutes or until potatoes are tender. Reduce heat to low and stir in soup, sour cream and milk.

Continue cooking. Stir occasionally until heated through.

Yield; 4-6 servings

EASY CLAM CHOWDER

½ cup chopped green onion
1 tablespoon butter
½ teaspoon cayenne pepper
3 strips diced bacon
3 minced garlic cloves
1 cup diced celery
2 cups diced carrots
1 cup undrained whole kernel corn
3–4 cups drained clams
1 8–ounce package cream cheese softened with clam juice
3 10¾–ounce cans cream of potato soup
1 10¾–ounce can cream of celery soup
2 soup cans milk

Cook first 5 ingredients until tender. In separate saucepan, cover celery and carrots with water and cook until tender; drain well. Add corn and clams; combine with first mixture. With electric mixer blend softened cream cheese, soups, and milk; combine all ingredients. Simmer, stirring frequently, until thoroughly heated.

Yield: 8–10 servings

ANN'S MIDWEST CHOWDER

- 2 cups boiling water
- 2½ cups chopped potatoes
- 1½ cups sliced carrots
- 1½ cups sliced celery
- ¼ cup chopped onion
- 1½ teaspoons salt
- ¼ teaspoon pepper
- ¼ cup margarine
- ¼ cup flour
- 2 cups milk
- 2½ cups shredded sharp Cheddar cheese
- 1 17–ounce can cream style corn

In large pot, combine water, vegetables and seasoning. Cover and simmer 10 minutes. Do not drain. Make a white sauce with margarine, flour and milk. Add cheese; stir until melted. Add corn and undrained vegetables. Heat thoroughly; do not boil.

Yield: 6–8 servings

Note: For variety, add one cup cooked cubed ham, chicken or turkey.

JACK'S HEARTY BEAN SOUP

- 1 pound ground chuck
- 3 medium finely chopped onions
- 1 chopped garlic clove
- 1 tablespoon brown sugar
- 1 teaspoon salt
- ½ teaspoon black pepper
- 2 tablespoons prepared mustard
- 1 15–ounce can lima beans
- 1 15–ounce can pinto beans
- 1 15–ounce can navy beans

Brown ground chuck in covered Dutch oven; add onion and garlic and cook until onion is transparent. Drain beans, reserving liquid. Thoroughly mix all ingredients; simmer for 30 minutes to allow flavors to mingle. Add liquid from beans as needed for desired consistency.

Yield: 6–8 servings

 *There are 250,000 species of flowering plants.*

VELVET CHEESE SOUP

¼ cup butter
½ cup diced onions
½ cup diced carrots
½ cup diced celery
¼ cup flour
1½ tablespoons cornstarch
2 14½–ounce cans chicken broth
2 cups milk
¼ cup butter
⅛ teaspoon baking soda
1 16–ounce box American deluxe cheese
salt and pepper to taste

Melt butter in large pot. Add vegetables and cook until soft. Add flour and cornstarch and cook until mixed. Add broth and milk slowly, stirring until smooth. Add soda and cheese. Do not boil.

Yield: 8 servings

CREAMY CHICKEN CHEESE SOUP

4 skinless, boneless chicken breast halves
3 cups water
⅓ cup chopped onion
½ cup chopped celery
2½ cups chopped carrots
2 10¾–ounce cans cream of chicken soup
1 cup milk
½ cup shredded American cheese

In covered saucepan, simmer chicken in water for about 20 minutes or until tender. Remove chicken, cool slightly, and dice. Add onion, celery and carrots to broth. Cover and simmer about 10 minutes. Gradually stir in the soup and milk; add chicken and cheese.

Yield: 8 servings

Note: For variations, add a package of frozen noodles to broth while vegetables are simmering; or add a 10–ounce package frozen mixed vegetables to broth.

CREAMY CORN SOUP

4 slices bacon
1 thinly sliced medium onion
1 cup diced raw potatoes
¼ teaspoon salt
1 16–ounce can whole kernel corn
1½ cups milk
1 10¾–ounce can cream of chicken soup

In large saucepan, cook bacon until crisp. Remove bacon and add liquid from corn to bacon drippings. Add onion, potatoes and salt to liquid and simmer until vegetables are tender. Add corn, milk and soup; heat thoroughly. Pour soup into bowls and garnish with crumbled bacon.

Yield: 6 servings

MEXICAN CORN SOUP

2 10½–packages frozen corn
1 15–ounce can chicken broth
¼ cup margarine
2 cups milk
1 minced garlic clove
1 teaspoon crushed dried oregano
1 4–ounce can chopped green chilies
1 16–ounce can diced tomatoes
1 cup cubed Monterey Jack cheese
1 whole cooked shredded chicken breast
2 tablespoons minced parsley
2 cups crushed corn chips

Thaw corn; combine corn and chicken broth in blender and purée. In large saucepan, combine margarine and corn. Simmer 5 minutes, stirring frequently. Add milk, garlic, oregano; bring to a boil. Reduce heat and add chilies; simmer 5 minutes. Add chicken and tomatoes; simmer 2 minutes. Remove from heat; add cheese. Ladle into bowls; garnish with parsley and crushed corn chips.

Yield: 6 servings

LENTIL SOUP

1½ cups dried lentils
5 slices finely chopped bacon
1 cup chopped onion
2 cups chopped celery
1 cup diced carrots
½ finely chopped garlic clove
2 cups diced potatoes
½ cup tomato purée
2 whole cloves
2 bay leaves
6 cups cold water
4 cups beef stock
1 tablespoon salt
dash white pepper
2 tablespoons red wine vinegar

Cover lentils with water; soak overnight; drain. In a 6 quart pot, sauté bacon lightly; add onion, celery, carrots and garlic; cook a few minutes. Add lentils, potatoes, tomato purée, cloves, bay leaves, water, beef stock, salt and pepper. Simmer covered for about 1½ hours. Add vinegar, more salt and pepper to taste.

Yield: 10–12 servings

Note: Wonderful with thinly sliced garlic sausage added to soup. Serve with crusty French bread.

DAD'S THICK VEGETABLE SOUP

1 pound ground beef
3 cloves minced garlic
1 teaspoon oregano
½ teaspoon cumin
2 14½–ounce cans beef consommé
1 large finely chopped onion
4 shredded potatoes
6 shredded carrots
5 chopped ribs celery with leaves
1½ teaspoons salt
¼ teaspoon pepper
1 28–ounce can whole tomatoes in purée

Brown beef with garlic. Add 1 cup water, oregano, cumin and consommé. Simmer about 1 hour. Chop tomatoes, fill cans with water, stir in remaining ingredients and add to beef mixture. Bring to boil and simmer an additional 15 minutes.

Yield: 12 servings

TACO SOUP

- **2 pounds browned lean ground beef**
- **1 teaspoon salt**
- **½ teaspoon pepper**
- **1 medium chopped onion**
- **1 4–ounce can undrained diced green chilies**
- **1 1¼–ounce package taco seasoning mix**
- **1 1–ounce package Ranch dressing mix**
- **3 14½–ounce cans undrained stewed tomatoes**
- **1 14½–ounce can undrained corn or hominy**
- **1 15–ounce can undrained kidney beans**
- **1 15–ounce can undrained pinto beans**
- **1½ cups water**
- **2 teaspoons ground cumin**

Brown beef and onion. Stir in remaining ingredients; bring to boil. Simmer 30 minutes or longer.

Yield: 10–12 servings

 *There are more than 8,500 species of birds.*

MOM'S BEEF STEW

- **2 pounds stew beef**
- **1 medium sliced onion**
- **6 beef bouillon cubes**
- **1 tablespoons dry parsley salt and pepper to taste Kitchen Bouquet**
- **2 14½–ounce cans whole potatoes**
- **1 14½–ounce can sliced carrots**

Place meat, onions, bouillon cubes, and parsley in large pot; cover with water. Bring to boil. Reduce heat, cover and simmer until beef is "falling apart" tender; add water, if necessary. Whip together water and flour and thicken gravy. Season with salt and pepper and add dash of Kitchen Bouquet for color. Drain vegetables; cut potatoes into bite–size cubes and add to stew. Heat thoroughly.

Yield: 6–8 servings

Note: May be frozen after beef cooks tender. Thaw and follow recipe to serve.

MICKEY'S CRABMEAT SANDWICH

- ½ cup chili sauce
- 1 3–ounce package softened cream cheese
- 1 cup King Crabmeat
- ½ teaspoon horseradish
- ½ teaspoon Worcestershire sauce
- 1 teaspoon chopped onion
- 2 teaspoons lemon juice
- 4 round buns
- ½ cup grated Cheddar cheese

Mix chili sauce with softened cream cheese; add remaining ingredients except grated cheese. Spread open–face on buns. Sprinkle with cheese and broil.

Yield: 8 servings

CUCUMBER FINGER SANDWICHES

- 4 cucumbers
- 2 8–ounce packages cream cheese
- 1 grated garlic clove
- 1 tablespoon onion juice
- 1 teaspoon sugar
- 1 teaspoon salt
- ¼ teaspoon Worcestershire sauce
- ½ cup mayonnaise
- ½ cup chopped nuts
- celery salt and paprika to taste

Peel and grate cucumbers. Blend cream cheese with all ingredients except nuts. Mix well and fold in nuts. Refrigerate overnight. Cut crusts from bread slices and spread with cucumber mixture. Cut into desired shapes.

Yield: 24 servings

Note: This recipe freezes well.

REGGIE'S TREATS

- 1 cup chopped black olives
- ½ cup thinly sliced green onions
- 1½ cups shredded Cheddar cheese
- ½ cup mayonnaise
- ½ teaspoon seasoned salt
- ½ teaspoon curry powder
- 8 English muffin halves

Mix first six ingredients. Spread on English muffin halves. Broil open face until cheese melts.

Yield: 8 servings

Note: This spread keeps well for several days in refrigerator.

GRILLED LIME CHICKEN ON RED CHILI BUNS

RED CHILI BUNS:

- **1 loaf frozen whole wheat bread dough**
- **1 can chipotle chilies in adobe sauce**
- **flour for kneading**

Thaw dough and warm to room temperature. Knead chilies into bread dough, using flour as needed. Cut dough into 8 equal pieces and shape into bun on ungreased baking sheet. Cover and allow to rise in warm place until double in size. Bake at 350 degrees 15–20 minutes or until lightly browned. Cool and slice in half just before serving.

LIME CHICKEN:

- **1 can chipotle chilies**
- **3 tablespoons soy sauce**
- **1 chopped serrano chili pepper**
- **½ cup orange juice**
- **½ cup lime juice**
- **2 tablespoons chopped garlic**
- **2 tablespoons white wine vinegar**
- **1½ teaspoons oregano**
- **1 teaspoon chili powder**
- **1 teaspoon ground cumin**
- **¼ teaspoon salt**
- **¼ teaspoon black pepper**
- **2 tablespoons chopped fresh cilantro**
- **8 boneless, skinless chicken breasts**

Combine all ingredients in plastic bag with chicken breasts. Marinate in refrigerator overnight. Grill marinated chicken breasts over high heat 4–5 minutes per side or until no longer pink in thickest part. Serve on red chili bun with tomato slice, red onion and cilantro mayonnaise.

CILANTRO MAYONNAISE:

- **1 cup fat free mayonnaise**
- **2 tablespoons chopped fresh cilantro**

Mix together and spread on buns.

Yield: 8 servings

TANGY FINGER SANDWICHES

- **1 8-ounce package softened cream cheese**
- **1 tablespoon onion juice**
- **¼ cup milk**
- **1 tablespoon chives**
- **1 teaspoon lemon juice**
- **1 loaf multi-grain bread**

Mix first five ingredients until well blended. Cut crusts off bread and spread filling on one slice, topping with one slice. Cut into three finger sandwiches.

Yield: 24 servings

ITALIAN HOAGIE SANDWICH

- **1 large sliced onion**
- **1 sliced bell pepper**
- **2 tablespoons zesty Italian salad dressing**
- **4 French sandwich rolls**
- **½ pound thinly sliced turkey or turkey pastrami**
- **4 slices Swiss cheese**
- **4 slices tomato**
- **mustard (any flavor)**

Sauté onion and green pepper in salad dressing until tender. Open French rolls and spread with mustard. Layer meat, cheese and tomato. Top with onions and bell pepper. Wrap each sandwich in foil and heat at 350 degrees for 15–20 minutes.

Yield: 4 servings

VEGGIE TEA SANDWICHES

- **1 8–ounce package softened cream cheese**
- **1 tablespoon lemon juice**
- **½ cup grated carrots**
- **¼ cup finely chopped celery**
- **¼ cup finely chopped green pepper**
- **¼ cup seeded and grated cucumber**
- **mayonnaise**
- **salt and pepper**
- **any variety sandwich bread**

Squeeze vegetables dry; mix together with softened cream cheese and lemon juice. Add mayonnaise for desired spreading consistency and salt and pepper to taste. Spread on bread slices, top with bread slice. Trim crusts and cut sandwiches into desired shapes.

Yield: 20 servings

Note: Freezes well.

HAWAIIAN DELIGHT

- **2 6–ounce cans drained fancy white crabmeat**
- **3 tablespoons finely diced red pepper**
- **3 tablespoons finely diced green pepper**
- **3 tablespoons finely diced onion**
- **¾ cup finely diced celery**
- **6 tablespoons drained crushed pineapple**
- **2 finely diced hard–boiled eggs**
- **3 tablespoons mayonnaise**
- **3 tablespoons Thousand Island dressing**
- **white pepper to taste**
- **1 loaf sandwich bread**

Mix all ingredients and blend well. Serve on whole wheat, rye or pumpernickel sandwich bread.

Yield: 8 servings

MANGO CHUTNEY

4 cups chopped mango
1⅓ cups chopped onion
1 garlic clove
1⅓ cups chopped red pepper
1 15-ounce box golden raisins
2 cups brown sugar
2 cups white vinegar
1 tablespoon mustard seed
1 tablespoon ground ginger
1 teaspoon ground allspice
1 teaspoon salt

Combine all ingredients in a large kettle. Slowly, bring to a boil and cook over low heat about 30 minutes or until thick. Pour into sterilized half-pint canning jars and seal. Process in hot water bath 10 minutes.

Yield: 8 half-pint jars

JOAN'S BREAD & BUTTER PICKLES

1 gallon thinly sliced unwaxed cucumbers
3 medium thinly sliced onions
2 shredded green bell peppers
½ cup salt
6 cups crushed ice

SYRUP:
4 cups sugar
4 cups white vinegar
1½ teaspoons turmeric
½ teaspoon ground cloves
2 tablespoons mustard seed
1 teaspoon celery seed

Put cucumbers, onions and peppers in a large bowl. Mix in salt and cracked ice. Let stand 3 hours. Drain well in colander and let stand 30 minutes. Mix syrup ingredients in a 6 quart pot. Add cucumber mixture and stir well. Heat to scalding, but do not boil. Immediately place in sterilized pint canning jars and seal.

Yield: 6 pints

There are 500,000 plant species in the world.

MARY WILL'S WONDERFUL DILLS

- **1 32-ounce jar hamburger dill slices**
- **1 cup sugar**
- **1 heaping teaspoon peppercorns**
- **1 cinnamon stick**

Drain juice from pickle jar, leaving 3 tablespoons juice in jar. Add remaining ingredients; shake jar until sugar is partially dissolved; refrigerate. During next 24 hours, shake jar to dissolve sugar; invert jar. Repeat process until all sugar is dissolved. Keeps indefinitely in refrigerator.

Yield: 1 quart

YAHOO! PICKLES

- **1 gallon sliced and drained dill pickles**
- **1 5-pound bag granulated sugar, less 1½ cups**
- **½ small bottle Tabasco sauce**
- **2-3 garlic cloves**

In large pickle jar, layer pickles, sugar, Tabasco and garlic. Put lid on jar securely and turn every day until sugar has dissolved, usually about 5 days. May be put in small jars at this time, if desired.

Yield: 6 pints

Note: These make wonderful gifts. Pack in pint jars and wrap with red bandana handkerchief; tie with raffia or jute. Your friends will shout, "Yahoo!"

CONNIE'S CROOKNECK SQUASH PICKLES

- **2 pounds firm fresh squash**
- **2 small onions**
- **¼ cup salt**
- **2 cups granulated sugar**
- **1 teaspoon celery salt**
- **1 teaspoon turmeric**
- **2 teaspoons mustard seeds**
- **3 cups cider vinegar**

Wash squash and cut into ⅛ to ¼ inch slices. Peel onion and slice very thin; add to squash. Cover squash and onions with water and salt; let stand 2 hours. Drain. Add remaining ingredients and bring to a boil and cook 5 minutes. Pack into hot sterilized jars, leaving ½ inch head space. Top with hot boiled lids. Screw rings on securely. When properly sealed, you will hear a "ping" and lids are depressed.

Yield: 6 pints

CRISP ZUCCHINI PICKLES

5 pounds zucchini squash
3 medium thinly sliced onions
½ cup canning/pickling salt
Ice cubes
3 cups 5% acid strength cider vinegar
3 cups granulated sugar
2 teaspoons celery seeds
2 teaspoons mustard seeds
1½ teaspoons turmeric
1 teaspoon ginger
1 teaspoon pepper

Wash zucchini and trim ⅛ inch off each end. Cut into ⅛ to ¼ inch slices. Combine zucchini, onions and salt in large bowl. Top with layer of ice; cover and let stand 3 hours. Drain and rinse in cold water. Combine zucchini mixture with vinegar, sugar and spices in a large kettle. Heat to boiling; reduce heat and simmer for 2 minutes. Ladle into hot sterilized pint jars to within ¼ inch of jar top. Wipe jar rim and top with hot boiled jar lids. Screw rings on securely. Jars are properly sealed when you hear a "ping" and lids are depressed.

Yield: 6 pints

CABBAGE–SWEET ONION RELISH

6 medium sweet onions
2 cups shredded cabbage
1 finely chopped red bell pepper
1 tablespoon mustard seeds
1 tablespoon celery seeds
1½ teaspoons salt
2½ cups sugar
1½ cups cider vinegar

Peel onions and cut into wedges; pulse in food processor until finely chopped; place in saucepan and add remaining ingredients. Cook very slowly 2 to 3 hours, stirring occasionally.

Yield: 3 pints

MANGO SALSA

2 peeled and diced mangos
½ cup diced red bell pepper
½ cup diced jícama
1 seeded and diced jalapeño
½ cup diced red onion
½ cup chopped fresh cilantro (optional)
¼ cup fresh lime juice
1 tablespoon honey
1 tablespoon wine vinegar

Combine all ingredients and marinate in refrigerator 2 to 3 hours. Serve with corn chips or favorite cracker.

Yield: 2 cups

HONEY MUSTARD SAUCE

⅓ cup mayonnaise
⅓ cup prepared salad dressing
2 tablespoons honey
1 tablespoon yellow mustard
1 teaspoon brown mustard

Mix and chill.

Yield: 1 cup

HOT MUSTARD SAUCE

1 cup tarragon vinegar
1 cup dry mustard
1 cup sugar
3 eggs

Mix vinegar and mustard in medium bowl and marinate overnight. Add sugar and eggs to marinated mixture; beat well with whisk. Pour mixture into top of double–boiler and cook over medium heat, stirring constantly, for 10 minutes or until thick. Remove from heat. Immediately pour into jars. Let cool completely; add lids. Store in refrigerator.

Yield: 24 ounces

BEST OF THE BEST MAYONNAISE

- 1 lemon
- 3 egg yolks
- ½ teaspoon dry mustard
- ¼ teaspoon salt
- pinch of cayenne or white pepper
- ¾ cup vegetable oil

Squeeze juice from lemon; strain; set aside. Beat egg yolks until thick and creamy; beat in lemon juice; add mustard, salt and pepper. Mix in vegetable oil, beating constantly until desired consistency. Refrigerate.

Yield: 1 cup

Note: Do not use olive oil. On garden fresh tomatoes, this mayonnaise is the "Best of the Best!"

 *A tree will die if the bark is stripped off all around the trunk.*

AUNT BONNIE'S SEASONED SALT

- 1 26-ounce box salt
- 1½ ounces black pepper
- 2 ounces cayenne pepper
- 1 ounce garlic powder
- 1 ounce chili powder
- 1 teaspoon thyme

Mix well.

Yield: 2 cups

Note: Spicy like a Cajun seasoning. Excellent with fish and chicken. Share with friends. They will ♥ you for it!

Salads & Dressings

SUNSHINE SALAD

- 1½ 6–ounce cans grapefruit sections in light syrup, broken into small pieces
- 1½ 11–ounce cans mandarin orange sections
- 3 tablespoons lemon juice
- dash of salt
- 1½ cups chopped walnuts
- 1 6–ounce package lemon gelatin
- 1 3–ounce package lemon gelatin

Dissolve gelatin in 3 cups hot water. Add juice from fruit (2 cups of juice). Add grapefruit, orange sections, lemon juice and nuts. Pour into 9x13 inch pan and chill till firm.

Yield: 8–10 servings

PINEAPPLE GELATIN SALAD

- 1 20–ounce can crushed pineapple
- 1 6–ounce package lemon flavored gelatin
- 3 cups boiling water
- 1 8–ounce package softened cream cheese
- 1 16–ounce carton frozen whipped topping
- ¾ cup sugar
- 3 tablespoons lemon juice
- 3 tablespoons water
- 2 tablespoons all purpose flour
- 2 lightly beaten egg yolks

Drain pineapple, reserving juice. Dissolve gelatin in water; add pineapple. Pour into a 9x13 inch glass dish; chill until almost set, about 45 minutes. In a mixing bowl, beat cream cheese and whipped topping until smooth. Carefully spread over gelatin; chill for 30 minutes. Meanwhile, in a saucepan over medium heat, combine sugar, lemon juice, water, flour, egg yolks and reserved pineapple juice; bring to a boil, stirring constantly. Cook 1 minute or until thickened. Cool. Carefully spread over cream cheese layer. Chill for at least 1 hour.

Yield: 12–16 servings

RASPBERRY PATCH SALAD

1 3–ounce box raspberry gelatin
2 envelopes plain gelatin
1 cup boiling water
1 10–ounce package frozen whole raspberries
1½ cups sour cream
1 3–ounce package pecan pieces
1 3–ounce package cherry gelatin
1 cup boiling water
1 20–ounce can crushed pineapple
1 16–ounce can whole berry cranberry sauce
lettuce

Dissolve raspberry gelatin and one envelope plain gelatin in 1 cup water. Add raspberries and stir until thawed. Pour into 9x13 inch dish. Chill until firm. Spread sour cream and nuts over first layer. Dissolve cherry gelatin and one envelope plain gelatin in 1 cup boiling water. Add drained pineapple and cranberry sauce and slightly chill. Pour over sour cream mixture and chill. Cut into squares and serve on lettuce leaves.

Yield: 12 servings

RASPBERRY–CRANBERRY SALAD

1 6–ounce package raspberry or cherry gelatin
1 cup boiling water
1 8–ounce can crushed pineapple
1½ tablespoons lemon juice
1 12–ounce container cranberry–orange relish
1 cup diced apples
½ cup broken pecans
½ cup finely chopped celery

Dissolve gelatin in one cup boiling water; add enough water to juice drained from pineapple to make one cup; stir into gelatin mixture. Add lemon juice; chill until slightly thickened. Fold in pineapple, cranberry–orange relish, apples, pecans and celery. Use 9x13 inch glass dish. Chill overnight.

Yield: 10–12 servings

The name amphibian means having two lives ...because they live in the water and on land.

RASPBERRY–BLUEBERRY SALAD

1 6–ounce box raspberry gelatin
2 cups boiling water
1 21–ounce can blueberry pie filling
1 20–ounce can crushed pineapple, NOT drained

Dissolve gelatin in boiling water. Let cool. Add pie filling and pineapple. Pour into 9x13 glass dish and congeal in refrigerator.

TOPPING:
1 8–ounce package softened cream cheese
1 cup sour cream
½ cup sugar
1 teaspoon vanilla flavoring
¼ cup chopped pecans (optional)

Combine cream cheese and sour cream. Add sugar and vanilla, beat thoroughly. Spread over congealed salad. Sprinkle with pecans over top if desired.

Yield: 8–10 servings

Variation: strawberry or cherry pie filling.

SALAD DEABATICOQUE

1 20–ounce can crushed pineapple
2 3–ounce packages apricot flavored gelatin
1 16–ounce can whole cranberry sauce
3 tablespoons lemon juice
1 teaspoon grated lemon peel
¼ teaspoon ground nutmeg
1 16–ounce carton sour cream
½ cup chopped pecans

Drain and add pineapple juice to gelatin in saucepan. Stir in 1 cup water. Heat to boiling. Remove from heat and stir in cranberry sauce, lemon peel and nutmeg. Chill mixture until slightly thickened, then add pineapple and nuts. Pour into a 1½ quart mold or 9x13 glass dish.

Yield: 8 servings

MYSTERY SALAD

3 3-ounce packages raspberry gelatin
1¼ cups hot water
3 1-pound cans stewed tomatoes
6 drops Tabasco sauce
1 head of lettuce
1 pint sour cream
1 tablespoon creamed horseradish
½ teaspoon salt
½ teaspoon sugar

Dissolve gelatin in hot water. Stir in tomatoes and Tabasco. Pour into lightly oiled 12 cup ring mold. Chill until firm. Unmold on a bed of lettuce. Mix last four ingredients and put in center of ring.

Yield: 10–12 servings

5TH AVENUE SALAD

1¼ cups orange juice
1 3-ounce package raspberry gelatin
1 12-ounce container cranberry-orange sauce
1 cup whipping cream or 2 cups whipped topping
1 medium chopped apple

Boil orange juice and dissolve gelatin into it. Add cranberry-orange sauce and partially chill. Beat cream until soft peaks form. Fold into mixture and add chopped apple pieces. Pour into 1 quart dish and chill for at least 6 hours.

Yield: 6–8 servings

VERNA'S CRANBERRY SALAD

1 6-ounce box cherry gelatin
2 cups boiling water
1 16-ounce can whole cranberry sauce
1 16-ounce carton sour cream
1 cup chopped nuts

Dissolve gelatin in boiling water; add cranberry sauce. Pour into 9x13 glass dish that has been sprayed with no stick cooking spray. Let stand in refrigerator until syrupy. Stir in sour cream and pecans. Congeal until set in refrigerator.

Yield: 8–10 servings

CHERRY RIBBON SALAD

- **1¼ cups boiling water**
- **1 3–ounce package cherry gelatin**
- **1 21–ounce can cherry pie filling**
- **1 cup boiling water**
- **1 3–ounce package orange–pineapple gelatin**
- **1 8¼–ounce can crushed pineapple**
- **⅓ cup mayonnaise**
- **1 cup whipped topping**
- **¼ cup chopped pecans**

Pour 1¼ cups boiling water and cherry gelatin into bowl, and stir until gelatin is dissolved. Stir in pie filling and pour into a 7 x 11 inch glass dish. Refrigerate until firm. Meanwhile pour 1 cup boiling water and orange–pineapple gelatin in bowl, and stir until gelatin is dissolved. Stir in crushed pineapple. Cool slightly but not set. Mix mayonnaise and whipped topping together and add to pineapple mixture. Add pecans and pour over cherry layer. Refrigerate until firm.

Yield: 6–8 servings

PRETZEL STRAWBERRY SALAD

FIRST LAYER:

- **2 cups broken thin pretzels**
- **¾ cup melted margarine**
- **3 tablespoons sugar**

Mix all 3 ingredients and spread on bottom of 9x13 inch pan. Bake 6–7 minutes at 400 degrees, let cool.

SECOND LAYER:

- **1 8–ounce package softened cream cheese**
- **1 cup sugar**
- **2 cups frozen whipped topping**

Mix and spread over first layer.

THIRD LAYER:

- **1 6–ounce package strawberry gelatin**
- **2 cups boiling water**
- **2 10–ounce packages frozen strawberries**

Mix strawberry gelatin with boiling water. Add frozen strawberries including juice. Refrigerate until mixture begins to congeal, then pour over second layer. Return to refrigerator until completely cool.

Yield: 8–10 servings

APRICOT SALAD

1 6–ounce box apricot gelatin
1 package unflavored gelatin
½ cup cold water
2 15¼–ounce cans sliced apricots
1 20–ounce can crushed pineapple
1 pint sour cream

Dissolve gelatins in ½ cup cold water. Drain juice from apricots and crushed pineapple and add enough water to make 3 cups. Heat in large pan until boiling. Remove from heat, add gelatin, fruit, and sour cream. Pour into 9 x 13 inch dish and refrigerate. Congeal.

Yield: 12–16 servings

 *A bee beats its wings about 200 times a second.*

MARCY'S MANDARIN TEA SALAD

1 15¼–ounce can crushed pineapple
1 11–ounce can mandarin oranges
1 Soothing Moments Orange and Spice tea bag
1½ tea cups hot water
1 6–ounce package orange gelatin
1 8–ounce can finely chopped water chestnuts

Drain pineapple and oranges and reserve juices. Add enough water to measure 1½ cups. Make tea with hot water and tea bag. Dissolve gelatin in hot tea and add the reserved juice liquid to tea and slightly chill. Fold in pineapple, oranges and water chestnuts. Spoon into 9 inch square pan and chill.

DRESSING:

½ cup mayonnaise
¼ cup heavy cream
1 tablespoon grated orange rind
¼ teaspoon mace
1 teaspoon sugar

Combine all ingredients and serve with salad.

Yield: 9 servings

SIN-APPLE SWIRL SALAD

½ cup red cinnamon candies
1 cup boiling water
2 3-ounce packages lemon gelatin
1 tablespoon unflavored gelatin
2 cups boiling water
2 cups applesauce
1 tablespoon lemon juice
1½ cups chopped walnuts
2 3-ounce packages softened cream cheese
¼ cup light cream
2 tablespoons salad dressing

Dissolve candies in 1 cup boiling water. Dissolve gelatins in 2 cups boiling water. Combine and stir in applesauce and lemon juice. Partially chill and add half of the nuts. Pour into 8x8 glass dish which is lightly greased. Blend remaining ingredients until smooth and swirl through salad. Chill and top with remaining nuts.

Yield: 8–12 servings

PINK PARTY SALAD

1 15-ounce can crushed pineapple
1 3-ounce box strawberry gelatin
1 16-ounce carton cottage cheese
1 cup heavy cream
½ cup chopped pecans

Drain pineapple juice into saucepan and add dry gelatin. Bring to a boil until dissolved. Remove from heat. Mix gelatin and reserved pineapple with cottage cheese and nuts. Whip heavy cream and fold into mold and congeal.

Yield: 6–8 servings

AVOCADO CONGEALED SALAD

1 3-ounce package lime gelatin
1 cup boiling water
1 8-ounce package softened cream cheese
¼ cup finely chopped green onion
¼ cup finely chopped green pepper
1 cup finely chopped celery
1 2-ounce jar chopped pimento
2 large chopped avocados
½ cup mayonnaise

Dissolve gelatin, add softened cream cheese and beat. Add all other ingredients except avocado and pimento. Chill 15–20 minutes, then add avocado and pimento. Chill until set.

Yield: 6–8 servings

CREOLE SALAD

- 1 6–ounce package lemon gelatin
- 1½ cups boiling water
- 1½ cups tomato juice
- 2 tablespoons chopped onion
- ½ cup chopped green pepper
- 2 tablespoons chopped pimentos
- 1 cup chopped cucumber
- ½ cup chopped celery
- 6 sliced hard boiled eggs (optional)
- lettuce

Dissolve gelatin in boiling water. Add tomato juice and chill slightly. Stir in next 5 ingredients and pour into 4 cup mold. Chill until firm. Serve on lettuce leaves topped with sliced eggs.

Yield: 6–8 servings

MANGO MOUSSE

- 1 14¾–ounce can mangoes
- 1 8–ounce package cream cheese
- 2 3–ounce boxes orange flavored gelatin
- 1 3–ounce box lemon flavored gelatin
- 2 cups boiling water

Place can of mangoes and cream cheese in a blender; blend until smooth. Dissolve gelatins in boiling water. Add blended mangoes and cream cheese. Pour into a 1½ quart mold. Chill until set. Serve in a ring 1½ quart bowl with strawberries in the center, or serve in squares, topped with curried mayonnaise.

Yield: 8 servings

Note: Apricots may be used instead of mangoes.

 *A mosquito beats its wings up to 500 times a second.*

ASHVILLE SALAD

- **1 10¾-ounce can tomato soup**
- **2 3-ounce packages cream cheese**
- **3 tablespoons unflavored gelatin**
- **¼ cup cold water**
- **1½ cups chopped celery**
- **1 chopped onion**
- **1 chopped green pepper**
- **1 cup mayonnaise**

Heat soup and stir in cream cheese. Dissolve gelatin in cold water and add to soup. Fold in vegetables and chill until firm. Whip mayonnaise into mixture and pour into individual molds or 8 inch square pan. Chill.

Yield: 8–10 servings

JUBILEE SALAD

- **1 10-ounce package frozen raspberries**
- **½ cup currant jelly**
- **2 cups water**
- **2 3-ounce packages raspberry gelatin**
- **½ cup sherry**
- **¼ cup lemon juice**
- **1 pound (2 cups) drained pitted dark cherries**

Thaw and drain raspberries, reserving syrup. Combine jelly and ½ cup water. Heat and stir until jelly melts. Add remaining 1½ cups water and the gelatin; heat and stir. Remove from heat. Add sherry, lemon juice, and reserved raspberry syrup. Chill until partially set. Fold raspberries and cherries into gelatin. Place into a 6 cup mold.

Yield: 8–10 servings

PISTACHIO SALAD

- **1 20-ounce can crushed pineapple**
- **1 3½-ounce package pistachio instant pudding**
- **2 cups small marshmallows**
- **½ cup chopped pecans**
- **1 8-ounce carton frozen whipped topping**

Mix all ingredients together and chill for at least 2 hours.

Yield: 6–8 servings

DIVINE PERFECTION SALAD

¼ cup cold water
1 envelope Knox gelatin
¼ cup sugar
½ teaspoon salt
1 cup hot water
¼ cup mild vinegar or rice vinegar
1 tablespoon lemon juice
½ cup finely chopped cabbage
1 cup finely chopped celery
1 chopped pimento or 2 tablespoons chopped green pepper

Pour cold water in bowl and add gelatin on top. Add sugar, salt and hot water and stir until dissolved. Add vinegar and lemon juice. Let cool until mixture begins to stiffen, then add remaining ingredients. Pour into 1½ quart mold that has been rinsed in cold water and chill. When firm, remove from mold to bed of lettuce leaves or endive and garnish with mayonnaise.

Yield: 6 servings

FAVORITE SUMMER SALAD

1 head red leaf lettuce
1 watermelon
1 avocado
1 fresh pineapple
1 pint package strawberries

Slice or chop into bite size pieces.

DRESSING:
½ cup sugar
1 teaspoon dry mustard
1 teaspoon salt
1 teaspoon celery salt
1 teaspoon paprika
1 teaspoon onion juice
¼ cup vinegar
1 cup oil

Mix vinegar and onion juice with dry ingredients. Add oil.

Yield: 8–10 servings

 *There are more insects on the earth than all other animals combined.*

SAUCY FRUIT SALAD

1 can drained mandarin oranges
1 20–ounce can drained pineapple chunks
3 sliced bananas
2 chopped red apples

FRUIT SAUCE:
1 3–ounce box sugar free instant vanilla pudding
1 cup skim milk
⅓ cup orange juice concentrate
1 6–ounce carton low fat banana yogurt

Mix fruit sauce ingredients and pour over fruit. Chill until ready to serve.

Yield: 8 servings

AVOCADO AND ORANGE SALAD

1½ large heads torn Romaine lettuce
1 11–ounce can drained mandarin oranges
2 sliced avocados

DRESSING:
⅔ cup salad oil
⅓ cup orange juice
2 tablespoons white vinegar
1 small garlic clove
1½ teaspoons basil
1 teaspoon sugar
¼ teaspoon salt and pepper to taste

Combine dressing ingredients in blender at least one hour before serving. Pour over the salad and toss lightly.

Yield: 8–10 servings

WALDORF SALAD

4 cups tart apples
1½ cups diagonal sliced celery
½ cup sour cream
¼ cup mayonnaise
1 teaspoon sugar
1 teaspoon vanilla
½ cup chopped walnuts

Cut apples into bite size pieces. Toss together apples, celery and nuts. Mix together sour cream, mayonnaise, sugar and vanilla. Refrigerate and chill before serving.

Yield: 8 servings

FRUITED SPINACH SALAD

2 Ruby red grapefruit
1 10–ounce bag torn spinach
1 pint cut strawberries

Mix together and use red wine vinaigrette as dressing.

Yield: 8–10 servings

ORANGE SPECIAL PEACHES

1 13–ounce can peach halves
1 teaspoon whole cloves
1 6 inch stick cinnamon
10 whole allspice
⅓ cup vinegar
½ cup sugar
1 sliced orange

Drain peaches and save ½ cup syrup. Put all spices in cloth or tea ball. In saucepan combine reserved peach syrup, vinegar, sugar, orange slices, peaches and spice bag. Heat to boiling. Simmer uncovered for 5 minutes. Cover and let cool to room temperature. Remove spice bag. Serve hot or cold.

Yield: 4–6 servings

SPICED PEACH HALVES

1 29–ounce can peach halves
¼ cup firmly packed brown sugar
½ teaspoon ground cinnamon
¼ teaspoon nutmeg
¼ cup melted and divided margarine
¼ cup crushed bran flakes or corn flakes
¼ cup coarsely chopped pecans
1 cup whipped topping
1 tablespoon molasses

Drain peaches, reserving ¼ cup juice. Put peaches, cut side up, in a shallow 1½ quart casserole. Combine peach juice, sugar, cinnamon, nutmeg, and 2 tablespoons margarine and spoon over peaches. Bake at 350 degrees for 10 minutes. Combine 2 tablespoons margarine, bran flakes and nuts. Sprinkle over peaches and bake at 400 degrees for 10 minutes. Combine whipped topping and molasses. Top peach halves and serve.

Yield: 6 servings

SEASONAL FRUIT SALAD

1 slightly beaten egg
juice from 15¼-ounce can pineapple tidbits
3 tablespoons flour
½ cup sugar
1 teaspoon lemon juice

Add beaten egg to pineapple juice in saucepan. Combine flour and sugar, then add to liquid in saucepan. Stir with wire whisk until smooth. Add lemon juice. Place over heat; bring to a boil; stirring constantly until mixture becomes like a paste. Let cool slightly before pouring over cut-up fruit in bowl. Coat fruit evenly. Chill.

Use over bananas, apples, grapes, mandarin oranges, cherries, pecans, etc.

Yield: 8 servings

Honeybees sometimes have as many as 80,000 members in a single colony.

THE BEST CONFETTI SALAD

1 15-ounce can seasoned green beans
1 15-ounce can shoe peg corn
1 15-ounce can peas
1 4.5-ounce jar sliced mushrooms
⅓ cup chopped green pepper
⅓ cup sliced celery
1 grated carrot
2 sliced green onions
1 minced clove garlic

DRESSING:
1 cup sugar
¾ cup white vinegar
½ cup vegetable oil
1 teaspoon mustard seed
½ teaspoon celery seed

Combine dressing ingredients and cook slowly until sugar is dissolved.

Drain first 4 ingredients and add to dressing. Cool until lukewarm. Pour over vegetables and chill. Will keep in refrigerator for several weeks. Better if made a day before serving.

Yield 10–12 servings

ITALIAN TOMATO SALAD

6 medium tomatoes
2 minced cloves garlic
2 tablespoons fresh basil (or ½ teaspoon dried)
¼ cup canola oil
salt and pepper to taste
Italian bread

Cut tomatoes in uneven chunks letting juice fall into bowl. Chop garlic and basil. Mix all ingredients. Marinate 2 hours.

Yield 4–5 servings

Note: Dip Italian bread into juice...delicious.

COTTAGE CHEESE SALAD IN ROMA TOMATOES

4 medium Roma tomatoes
2½ cups low fat cottage cheese
¼ cup chopped onions
¼ cup chopped green peppers
¼ cup chopped celery
2 tablespoons grated Parmesan cheese
⅛ teaspoon garlic powder

Cut tops from tomatoes and scoop out pulp. Chill. Combine remaining ingredients and chill. To serve, stuff tomatoes with cottage cheese mixture.

Yield: 4 servings

ORIENTAL PEA SALAD

1 10–ounce package frozen green peas
1 cup thinly sliced celery
¼ cup chopped green onions
¾ cup mayonnaise
2 tablespoons lemon juice
1 teaspoon curry powder
⅛ teaspoon garlic salt
1 teaspoon soy sauce
¼ cup toasted slivered almonds
1 cup crisp chow mein noodles

Combine mayonnaise, lemon juice, curry powder, garlic salt, and soy sauce. Add peas, celery and onions. Toss and chill. Add noodles and almonds at serving time. Toss lightly.

Yield: 6 servings

ANNETTE'S SALAD

1 15¼-ounce can green peas (may substitute rinsed black beans)
1 15¼-ounce can white shoe peg corn
2 14½-ounce green beans
1½ cups julienne sliced celery
2 thinly sliced red peppers (or green)
1 cup thinly sliced onion

DRESSING:
1 cup sugar
½ cup white vinegar
½ cup oil

Heat to boiling sugar, white vinegar and oil. Cool. Drain canned vegetables and toss with dressing. Marinate several hours or overnight before serving.

Yield: 6–8 servings

AUNT MARCY'S BROCCOLI–RAISIN SALAD

2 heads broccoli, flowerets
1 chopped small red onion
8 slices cooked crisp and crumbled bacon
½ cup raisins
½ cup hulled sunflower seeds

DRESSING:
1 cup salad dressing
½ cup sugar
4 tablespoons cider vinegar

Combine all ingredients with dressing and refrigerate overnight.

Yield: 8–10 servings

Note: For a good variation, add 1 cup shredded Cheddar.

CALIFORNIA BROCCOLI SALAD

1 large bunch broccoli
½ cup chopped red onion
1 pound fried crisp and crumbled bacon
½ cup sunflower seeds
1½ cups sliced red grapes

Cut broccoli into flowerets.

DRESSING:
1 cup mayonnaise
½ cup sugar or honey
2 tablespoons red wine vinegar

Mix first five ingredients. Mix in blender all dressing ingredients and pour over salad.

Yield: 8 servings

HEARD'S CHICKEN SALAD CRÊPES

4 cups cooked cubed chicken
1 cup sliced celery
1 8-ounce can drained pineapple tidbits
1 8-ounce can sliced and halved water chestnuts
1½ cups sliced in half seedless grapes
½ cup toasted slivered almonds
1 1-ounce package Hidden Valley dry salad mix
½ cup low fat yogurt
½ cup mayonnaise
½ cup honey

APRICOT SAUCE:
½ cup apricot jam
½ cup mayonnaise
1 or 2 teaspoons curry powder

Mix last four ingredients and mix with above ingredients and set aside. Add mixture to crêpes and cook according to crêpe recipe listed in the Bread Section. When crêpes are assembled, mix all sauce ingredients and drizzle over crêpes.

Yield: 8–10 servings

PARTY CHICKEN SALAD

- **12 cooked and boned fryers**
- **12 hard boiled and chopped eggs**
- **½ cup chopped parsley**
- **1 cup chopped sweet pickles**
- **2 teaspoons pepper**
- **6 cups mayonnaise**
- **1 cup chopped almonds**
- **3 heads lettuce**

Mix all ingredients together the night before serving. Serve on top cantaloupe wedges.

Yield: 50 servings

VINEYARD CHICKEN SALAD (AKA) CHICKEN FRUIT SALAD

- **4 cups cooked cubed chicken**
- **1 cup sliced celery**
- **1 8–ounce can drained pineapple tidbits**
- **1 8–ounce can sliced and drained water chestnuts**
- **1½ cups seedless sliced grapes**
- **½ cup slivered almonds**

DRESSING:

- **1 10–ounce package Hidden Valley salad dressing**
- **½ cup low fat yogurt**
- **½ cup mayonnaise**
- **½ cup honey**

Mix together and add dressing 30 minutes before serving.

Yield: 6–8 servings

ORIENTAL CHICKEN SALAD

- **4 cups diced cooked chicken breasts**
- **2 11–ounce cans mandarin oranges**
- **1 8–ounce can bamboo shoots**
- **1 5–ounce can sliced water chestnuts**
- **1 cup slivered almonds**
- **2 cups mayonnaise**
- **2 cups chow mein noodles**

Mix all ingredients except noodles. Chill. Just before serving add noodles. Serve on lettuce leaves.

Yield: 8 servings

TEA HOUSE CHICKEN SALAD

3 cups chopped chicken
6 chopped hard boiled eggs
1½ cups chopped celery
1 cup toasted chopped pecans
1½ cups chopped sweet pickles
1 cup plain yogurt
1 cup mayonnaise
salt and pepper to taste

Mix all ingredients and serve.

Yield: 8 servings

TANGY ORIENTAL GREEN BEAN SALAD

3 15–ounce cans cut green beans
1 4–ounce jar drained and sliced artichokes
1 7–ounce can drained and sliced mushrooms
1 8–ounce jar drained and chopped water chestnuts
1 4–ounce jar drained and diced pimentos
½ cup sliced green olives
2 tablespoons olive oil
1 tablespoon oregano
1 tablespoon parsley flakes
1 bunch sliced green onions
juice of 2 lemons

Combine all ingredients and chill.

Yield: 8–10 servings

COLD GREEN BEAN SALAD

1 15–ounce can green beans
1 unpeeled and sliced cucumber
1 thinly sliced onion
1 package dry garlic Good Seasons salad dressing mix
1 cup wine vinegar
1 cup vegetable oil
1 4.5–ounce can mushrooms

Make several layers of drained beans, onion slices, cucumber slices and mushrooms in a covered container. Mix salad dressing according to package directions and pour over vegetables. Let stand overnight in refrigerator, turning ingredients several times. Serve cold.

Yield: 4–6 servings

SOUTHWEST BEAN SALAD

- 1 15-ounce can kidney beans
- 1 15-ounce can black beans
- 1 15-ounce can northern beans
- 2 sliced celery ribs
- 1 diced medium red onion
- 1 diced medium tomato
- 1 11-ounce can corn

Drain and rinse canned beans and corn.

DRESSING:

- ¾ cup salsa
- ¼ cup vegetable oil
- ¼ cup lime juice
- ½ teaspoon chili powder
- ½ teaspoon salt
- ½ teaspoon ground cumin

Mix all ingredients, add dressing and mix well. Make day ahead. Chill.

Yield: 8–10 servings

YOUR CHOICE GREEN BEAN SALAD

- 2 16-ounce cans drained French cut green beans
- 1 can peas
- 1 can chopped artichoke hearts
- ½ cup sugar
- ½ cup white vinegar
- ½ cup vegetable oil
- 1 sliced medium purple onion
- ½ cup sliced water chestnuts
- 1 4-ounce jar sliced and drained pimento
- 4 slices fried and crumbled bacon

Place beans in shallow dish. Pour sugar, vinegar and oil over beans, artichokes and peas. Chill overnight or longer. Drain vegetables, add onion, water chestnuts and sliced pimento. Toss gently. Spoon into 2 quart casserole, sprinkle bacon over top and bake 30 minutes at 350 degrees. Serve hot or cold.

Yield: 6–8 servings

ORIENTAL WILD RICE SALAD

- **¼ cup wild rice**
- **1 cup chicken broth**
- **¼ cup brown rice**
- **3 tablespoons orange juice**
- **2 tablespoons rice vinegar or white vinegar**
- **1 tablespoon soy sauce**
- **¾ teaspoon toasted sesame oil**
- **½ teaspoon grated ginger root**
- **1 minced clove garlic**
- **1 11–ounce can mandarin orange sections**
- **1 8–ounce can chopped whole water chestnuts**
- **½ cup chopped red or green pepper**
- **2 tablespoons sliced green onion**
- **½ cups frozen peas**
- **spinach leaves**
- **1 tablespoon chopped cashews or peanuts**

Rinse wild rice in strainer under cold water. In a small saucepan, combine chicken broth, brown rice and wild rice. Bring to boiling, reduce heat and simmer, covered about 40 minutes or until rice is tender and liquid absorbed. Meanwhile, for dressing, combine orange juice, rice vinegar, soy sauce, sesame oil, ginger root, and garlic. Shake well. In a large bowl combine rice, drained mandarin orange sections, drained water chestnuts, sweet pepper and green onion. Pour dressing over rice mixture, toss lightly. Cover and chill for 4 to 24 hours. Just before serving, stir in thawed peas. Serve on spinach lined plates. Sprinkle each serving with cashews or peanuts.

Yield: 8 servings

CLASSIC BERMUDA SALAD

DRESSING:

- **1 cup salad oil**
- **½ cup tarragon vinegar**
- **2 teaspoons sugar**
- **1 teaspoon salt**
- **½ teaspoon paprika**

- **1 small head cauliflower, separated into flowerets**
- **½ thinly sliced large Bermuda onion, separated into rings**
- **⅓ cup sliced stuffed olives**
- **½ cup crumbled Roquefort cheese**
- **1 head lettuce**

Marinate dressing with cauliflower, onion and olives for 1 hour. Immediately before serving, add crumbled Roquefort cheese and one head lettuce. Toss well.

Yield: 8–10 servings

SWEET AND SOUR CUCUMBERS

½ cup white vinegar
⅓ cup salad oil
2 tablespoons sugar
1 teaspoon salt
¼ teaspoon white pepper
¼ teaspoon oregano leaves
3 thinly sliced medium cucumbers

About 1 hour before serving time or up to 2 days ahead, combine ingredients in small bowl. Refrigerate, stirring occasionally to blend flavors.

Yield: 6–8 servings

MARINATED SLAW

1 large shredded cabbage
1 onion, sliced into rings
1 cup sugar
¾ cup oil
1 cup vinegar
1 teaspoon mustard seed
1 teaspoon celery seed
1 tablespoon salt

Layer cabbage and onion in a bowl with lid. Heat next 6 ingredients to a boil and pour over cabbage and onions. Refrigerate for at least 4 hours or overnight. Shake cabbage from time to time.

Yield: 8–12 servings

SWEET AND SOUR RED CABBAGE

2–3 pounds shredded red cabbage
2 pared and grated apples
2 tablespoons butter
6–8 tablespoons wine vinegar
6–8 tablespoons water
salt and pepper to taste
5 tablespoons red currant jelly
2 tablespoons sugar

Melt butter. Add cabbage and apples. Cook and toss 5 minutes. Add vinegar, water, salt and pepper. Cook over low heat until tender. Add sugar and jelly. Bring to boil. Serve.

Yield: 10–12 servings

GIGI'S CABBAGE SALAD

1 head chopped green cabbage
2 cups chopped red cabbage
5 chopped green onions, with tops

Toss and refrigerate overnight in airtight container.

1 3–ounce package chicken flavored Ramen noodles (reserve seasoning packet)
½ cup slivered almonds
¼ cup butter

Break noodles in a baggie. Melt butter, brown noodles and almonds until brown. Drain and cool.

DRESSING:
½ cup oil
¼ cup white vinegar
½ teaspoon salt
½ cup sugar
1 seasoning packet from Ramen noodles

Beat above ingredients until sugar is dissolved. Chill. Before serving, toss noodles and almonds with cabbage and dressing.

Yield: 10 servings

OVERNIGHT CABBAGE SALAD

2 cups shredded cabbage
1 7–ounce can drained green peas
1 8–ounce can drained sliced water chestnuts
¼ cup chopped onion
¾ cup chopped celery
1 large chopped red apple
¼ teaspoon salt
½ cup sour cream
½ cup mayonnaise or salad dressing
1 teaspoon sugar
1 cup shredded Cheddar cheese
1 cup finely chopped pecans

Combine first 7 ingredients, toss well. Combine sour cream, mayonnaise and sugar. Stir until blended. Spread over cabbage mixture, sealing edges of bowl. Layer cheese and pecans on top. Cover and chill for 8 hours or overnight. Toss before serving.

Yield: 8–10 servings

CRUNCHY ALMOND SALAD

1 head lettuce
1 head Napa cabbage
1 bunch green onions (about 6)
½ cup margarine
2 3-ounce packages Ramen noodle soup mix (DO NOT use season packet)
1½ cups slivered almonds
3 tablespoons sesame seeds

DRESSING:
¾ cup sugar
1 cup salad oil
½ cup mild vinegar
3 tablespoons soy sauce

Mix together dressing ingredients and bring to a boil and cook until sugar melts. Cool. Shred cabbage and lettuce and place in large bowl. Finely slice onions and place in bowl. Brown almonds and sesame seeds in 350 oven about 5–10 minutes and place in bowl. Brown crunched up Ramen noodles in butter. Place in bowl. Pour cooled dressing over all and toss.

Refrigerate before serving.

Yield: 10–12 servings

SAUERKRAUT SALAD

2 16-ounce cans sauerkraut
1 large purple onion
1 large bell pepper
¾ cup sugar
¾ cup salad oil
1 cup vinegar
1 tablespoon celery seeds

Drain sauerkraut well. Slice onion and bell pepper thin. Bring sugar, oil, vinegar, and celery seeds to a boil, then pour over pepper, onion, and sauerkraut. Toss lightly and refrigerate overnight.

Yield: 12 servings

HEARTS OF PALM SALAD

- 1 head broken Iceberg lettuce
- 1 head broken Romaine lettuce
- 1 sliced small red onion
- 1 14–ounce can chopped plain artichoke hearts
- 1 14–ounce can chopped hearts of palm
- 1 4–ounce jar chopped pimentos
- ⅓ cup red wine vinegar
- ½ cup salad oil
- shredded Parmesan cheese

Combine all vegetables in large bowl. Toss with vinegar, oil and lots of cheese.

Yield: 10 servings

BOMBAY SPINACH SALAD

DRESSING:

- ¼ cup white wine vinegar
- ¼ cup canola oil
- 2 tablespoons chutney
- 2 teaspoons sugar
- ½ teaspoon salt
- 1 teaspoon curry powder
- 1 teaspoon dry mustard

- 1 bag fresh spinach
- 1½ cups chopped apples, both red and green skin
- ½ cup white raisins
- ½ cup peanuts
- 2 tablespoons chopped green onion

Combine all dressing ingredients. Mix torn, rinsed and drained spinach with remaining salad ingredients. Toss with dressing.

Yield: 10 servings

 *Bees perform special dances to show other members of the hive where to look for nectar outside the hive.*

YOUR CHOICE SPINACH MUSHROOM SALAD

DRESSING #1:

1 cup salad oil
¾ cup brown sugar
⅓ cup catsup
¼ cup vinegar
1 tablespoon Worcestershire sauce
1 small chopped onion

Blend in blender.

DRESSING #2:

½ cup white vinegar
½ cup apple cider vinegar
⅔ cup sugar
½ cup vegetable or corn oil
1 teaspoon salt
1 teaspoon pepper

Shake in jar until blended.

MIX:

1 or 2 packages fresh washed, dried and torn spinach
½ pound fresh sliced mushrooms
8 slices of crumbled crisp bacon
3 finely chopped hard-boiled eggs
1 15-ounce can drained bean sprouts (optional)

Add dressing just before serving or serve on the side. If desired, top with diced tomatoes after adding dressing.

Yield: 8 servings

FRESH SPINACH AND ORANGE SALAD

1 10-ounce package fresh spinach
½ sliced red onion
3 sectioned oranges
4 cooked and crumbled bacon strips

Remove stems from spinach, rinse and drain. Combine all ingredients.

DRESSING:

2 tablespoons cider vinegar
1 tablespoon sugar
¼ teaspoon salt
¼ teaspoon dry mustard
⅓ cup salad oil

Add dressing to spinach mixture and gently toss.

Yield: 8–10 servings

GRAPEFRUIT–STRAWBERRY SPINACH SALAD

2 ruby red grapefruit
1 10–ounce bag fresh rinsed and drained spinach
1 pint fresh sliced strawberries

Cut grapefruit, spinach and strawberries into bite–size pieces.

DRESSING:
1 8–ounce bottle red wine vinegar and oil dressing
½ cup sugar
½ teaspoon dry mustard
1½ teaspoons grated grapefruit peel
2 tablespoons poppy seeds
¼ cup grapefruit juice

Mix dressing ingredients, shaking well. Add to spinach and fruit just before serving.

Yield: 16 (¾ cup) servings

SPECIAL SPINACH SALAD

1 pound fresh spinach
1 16–ounce can bean sprouts
1 8–ounce can water chestnuts
3 hard boiled eggs
½ pound fried and diced crisp bacon
1 medium chopped onion

DRESSING:
1 cup salad oil
¾ cup brown sugar
¼ cup vinegar
⅓ cup catsup
1 tablespoon Worcestershire sauce

In a large salad bowl, place washed spinach, drained sprouts, drained and sliced water chestnuts, chopped hard boiled eggs, fried bacon and chopped onion. Blend together salad oil, sugar, vinegar, catsup and Worcestershire sauce and pour over spinach mixture. Toss lightly.

Yield: 6–8 servings

Note: One or two hard boiled eggs can be held aside and sliced over the top of the salad after dressing has been added and salad tossed.

PASTA VERDE

4 cups cooked spinach egg noodles
1 cup diced tomato
¼ cup finely chopped red pepper
¼ cup finely chopped green pepper
2 to 3 chopped green onions
½ cup chopped broccoli
1 cup shredded carrots
½ cup chopped celery

DRESSING:
½ cup mayonnaise
½ cup sour cream
1 teaspoon lemon juice
2 tablespoons milk
1 teaspoon Knorr's Seasoning for Meat
1 teaspoon parsley flakes
1 teaspoon onion salt
¼ teaspoon garlic powder
¼ teaspoon black pepper

Combine all ingredients listed. Mix well. Chill.

Yield: 10 (½ cup) servings

Note: One 12-ounce package of spinach noodles equals 2 recipes. Can be made a day ahead. Improves with overnight refrigeration. Serve on lettuce leaves.

JENNY'S POTATO SALAD

3 pounds new red potatoes
1 tablespoon vinegar

SAUCE:
1½ teaspoons red wine vinegar
2 tablespoons oil
1 teaspoon salt
1 teaspoon pepper
1 teaspoon garlic salt
1 cup diced celery
¾ teaspoon dill weed
2 teaspoons mustard
⅓ cup green onions
2 tablespoons honey
1 cup mayonnaise

Cook new red potatoes in water with vinegar, peel when cool. Mix sauce and stir carefully into potatoes. Chill.

Yield: 12 servings

MOM'S POTATO SALAD

- 1¼ cups mayonnaise
- 1 teaspoon prepared mustard
- ½ teaspoon celery seed
- ½ teaspoon salt
- ⅛ teaspoon pepper
- 4 cups cubed and peeled boiled potatoes (4 medium potatoes or 4 cups mashed potatoes)
- 2–4 chopped boiled eggs
- ½ cup chopped onion
- ½ cup sweet pickle relish

Combine all ingredients except potatoes and eggs; mix well. Add potatoes and eggs; mix well. Sprinkle top with paprika; chill.

Yield: 6–8 servings

HAM AND EGG SALAD

- 1 8-ounce package elbow macaroni
- 1 10-ounce package frozen peas
- 3 cups hard boiled eggs
- ¼ cup minced onion
- 1 cup diced Cheddar cheese
- 1 cup diced chicken
- 1 cup mayonnaise
- 1 teaspoon prepared mustard
- ¼ teaspoon salt
- ½ teaspoon sugar
- ¼ teaspoon pepper

Prepare macaroni according to package directions. Combine cooked macaroni, peas, ham, eggs, onion, cheese and chicken. Blend remaining ingredients. Toss all ingredients together and chill.

Yield: 6–8 servings

CRUNCHY VEGETABLE SALAD

- 1 cup oil
- 1 cup white sugar
- ½ cup vinegar
- 2 cups drained cut green beans
- 2 cups small English peas
- 1 8-ounce can sliced water chestnuts
- 2 cups thinly sliced celery
- 1 4-ounce jar chopped pimento
- head of lettuce

Mix oil, sugar and vinegar until blended. Add remaining ingredients and marinate overnight. Drain and serve on lettuce leaf.

Yield: 6–8 servings

ITALIAN MARINATED VEGETABLES

- **1 can drained whole mushrooms**
- **1 can drained cut in half artichoke hearts**
- **1 can ripe olives**
- **12 cherry tomatoes**
- **1 fresh cauliflower**
- **1 fresh bunch broccoli**
- **1 each red and yellow pepper**

Drain mushrooms and artichoke hearts. Cut cauliflower and broccoli into flowerets. Cut peppers into julienne strips.

MARINADE:

- **1 cup red wine vinegar**
- **⅔ cup olive oil**
- **¼ cup minced onions**
- **2 teaspoons dry Italian dressing mix**
- **1 teaspoon salt**
- **1 teaspoon garlic salt**
- **1 teaspoon onion salt**
- **1 teaspoon sugar**

Combine all marinade ingredients and bring to a boil. Pour hot marinade over the vegetables, except tomatoes. Refrigerate overnight. Stir occasionally. Add tomatoes for color 2 or 3 hours before serving. This is very pretty drained and served in a deep glass bowl; or serve as hors d'oeuvres with toothpicks.

Yield: 10–12 servings

QUICK VEGETABLE SALAD

- **1 bunch broccoli**
- **1 head cauliflower**
- **1 10–ounce package frozen peas**
- **1 cup chopped celery**
- **½ cup chopped onion**

Cut broccoli and cauliflower into flowerets.

SAUCE:

- **1 cup salad dressing**
- **½ cup sugar**
- **½ cup sour cream**
- **1 tablespoon Beau Monde seasoning**
- **1 tablespoon garlic salt**
- **1 teaspoon black pepper**

Mix sauce with vegetables and chill.

Yield: 12 servings

FROZEN AMBROSIA

- ¾ cup sugar
- 1 8-ounce package softened cream cheese
- 2 or 3 mashed bananas
- 1 10-ounce package thawed strawberries
- 1 10-ounce can crushed and drained pineapple tidbits
- ½ cup chopped pecans
- 1 16-ounce carton whipped topping

Cream sugar and cream cheese in large mixer bowl. Combine bananas, strawberries, pineapple and pecans in large bowl. Mix well. Add to creamed mixture. Fold in whipped topping. Pour into 9x13 inch glass pan. Freeze until firm.

Yield: 12 servings

SALAD LA PARISIENNE

- 2 cups thinly sliced cauliflower
- 1 cup broccoli
- 1 4½-ounce can drained and chopped ripe olives
- ⅓ cup chopped green pepper
- 1 4-ounce jar drained and chopped pimentos
- ¼ cup thinly sliced green onion

Mix together and toss with red wine vinaigrette dressing.

Yield: 10 half cup servings

BUTTONS AND BOWS CHICKEN SALAD

- 2 cups cooked and diced chicken breast
- 1½ cups diced celery
- 1 teaspoon grated onion
- 1 teaspoon salt
- ¼ teaspoon white pepper
- 1 teaspoon lemon juice
- ⅓ cup chopped pecans
- 1½ cups mayonnaise

TOPPING:

- ⅔ cup grated Cheddar cheese
- 1 cup finely crushed potato chips

Combine ingredients and spoon into a 9 inch pie shell. Combine topping ingredients and sprinkle on pie. Bake at 350 degrees for 20–25 minutes. Serve with lettuce or fruit salad and a croissant.

Yield: 8 servings

PUTTIN' ON THE RITZ CHICKEN SALAD

3 cups chopped cooked chicken
1 cup finely chopped celery
½ cup sliced almonds
½ cup crushed Ritz crackers
2 tablespoons finely chopped onion
1 10¾-ounce can cream of chicken soup
1 6-ounce can mushroom stems and pieces
½ cup mayonnaise (not salad dressing)

Mix above and top with mixture of:

1 4-ounce package crushed potato chips
1 10-ounce package grated Cheddar cheese

Spray 9x13 inch glass dish lightly with cooking spray. Bake uncovered in 325 degree oven for 30–45 minutes.

Yield: 8 servings

HOT CHICKEN SALAD

2 cups diced cooked chicken
2 cups diced celery
2 teaspoons grated onion
½ cup chopped toasted almonds
½ teaspoon Accent
2 tablespoons lemon juice
1 cup mayonnaise
½ teaspoon salt
2½ teaspoons tarragon vinegar
1 8-ounce can sliced water chestnuts
½ cup grated cheese
1 cup crushed potato chips
parsley

Combine all ingredients except cheese and chips. Place in well greased 9x13 inch casserole. Sprinkle with cheese, then chips. Bake 10 minutes at 450 degrees. Serve hot. Garnish with parsley.

Yield: 4–6 servings

Note: Freezes well.

CHICKEN SALAD ROLLS

- 1 8–ounce package cream cheese
- 4 tablespoons milk
- 2 tablespoons chopped onion
- 1 2–ounce jar chopped pimentos
- 2 tablespoons melted butter or oleo
- 4 cups chopped cooked chicken
- ½ teaspoon salt
- ¼ teaspoon pepper
- ½ teaspoon garlic powder
- ½ cup shredded Cheddar cheese
- 2 cans crescent rolls

Mix all ingredients except crescent rolls. Separate crescent rolls into 16 triangles. Place 2 tablespoons of salad on each triangle and wrap crescent roll around salad. Seal well. Place on cookie sheet and bake at 350 degrees for 30 minutes.

Yield: 8–10 servings

MEXICAN CHICKEN SALAD

- 8 whole cooked and boned chicken breasts
- 2 cups chunky salsa
- ¼ cup coarsely chopped green onion
- 1 peeled, seeded and chopped avocado
- 1 chopped tomato
- 1 3–ounce can sliced ripe olives
- 1 15–ounce can drained garbanzo beans
- garlic powder
- freshly ground black pepper
- 1 cup shredded Monterey Jack cheese
- tortilla chips (optional)

Cut chicken into 1–inch pieces and combine with salsa. Refrigerate overnight. When ready to serve, place in large bowl and layer ingredients, except cheese, over the chicken. Season to taste with garlic powder and pepper. Toss lightly. Top with cheese and serve with tortilla chips.

Soak avocado briefly in lemon juice and water to retain color. Salad is pretty served in individual edible tortilla baskets.

Yield: 8 servings

SPINACH CHICKEN SALAD

- 5 cups cubed cooked chicken (about 3 whole breasts)
- 2 cups green grape halves
- 1 cup snow peas
- 2 cups packed torn spinach
- 2½ cups sliced celery
- 1 7–ounce package cooked and drained corkscrew pasta or elbow macaroni
- 1 6–ounce jar drained and quartered marinated artichoke hearts
- ½ large sliced cucumber
- 3 sliced green onions with tops
- large spinach leaves (optional)
- orange slices (optional)

In large bowl, combine chicken, grapes, peas, celery, pasta, artichoke hearts, cucumber and green onions. Cover and refrigerate.

DRESSING:

- ½ cup vegetable oil
- ½ cup sugar
- 2 tablespoons white wine vinegar or rice vinegar
- 1 teaspoon salt
- ½ teaspoon dried minced onion
- 1 teaspoon lemon juice
- 2 tablespoons minced fresh parsley

Combine all dressing ingredients in a jar or small bowl; mix well and refrigerate. When cold, pour dressing over salad and toss. Refrigerate overnight. Toss with spinach right before serving.

Yield: 10–12 servings

STRAWBERRY CHICKEN SALAD

- 2 cups diced cooked chicken
- 1 cup thinly sliced celery
- 2 cups sliced fresh strawberries
- ⅔ cup salted cashew nuts

DRESSING:

- 1 cup mayonnaise
- ¼ teaspoon prepared mustard
- 4 tablespoons lemon juice
- ½ teaspoon salt

Toss gently just before serving.

Yield: 8–10 servings

FONDULOHA

- **2 8–ounce cans drained pineapple chunks**
- **2½ cups cubed cooked chicken**
- **¾ cup diced celery**
- **1 11–ounce can drained mandarin oranges**
- **¾ cup mayonnaise**
- **1 tablespoon curry powder**
- **1 medium sliced banana**
- **½ cup salted peanuts**
- **½ cup flaked coconut**

Combine cubed pineapple, chicken, celery and oranges. Cover and chill overnight. Mix mayonnaise and curry powder, cover and chill overnight. Toss before serving with coconut, peanuts and banana. Lightly toss with mayonnaise.

Yield: 8 servings

SEVEN LAYER MEXICAN SALAD

- **1 head shredded lettuce**
- **2–3 chopped fresh tomatoes**
- **1 small chopped red onion**
- **1 15–ounce can Ranch Style Chili Beans, juice included**
- **1 cup shredded Cheddar cheese**
- **1 9–ounce bag lightly crushed Frito chips**
- **1 8–ounce bottle 7 Seas Creamy Italian dressing or Kraft Catalina**

Layer in large bowl in order listed with dressing on top. May do ahead except for dressing. Do NOT mix up ingredients.

Yield: 8–10 servings

COLD PAELLA SALAD

- **1 6–ounce package frozen, cooked peeled and deveined shrimp**
- **3 cups cooked yellow rice pinch saffron, turmeric or paprika**
- **1 8–ounce can drained and minced clams**
- **½ cup diced cooked chicken**
- **1½ cups sliced celery**
- **1½ cups frozen cooked green peas**
- **½ cup diced green pepper**
- **⅓ cup sliced green onion with tops**
- **1 cup mayonnaise**
- **3 tablespoons capers (optional)**
- **½ teaspoon salt**
- **¼ teaspoon garlic powder**
- **¼ teaspoon black pepper**

Cook rice according to package directions in chicken broth with pinch of saffron, turmeric or paprika. Allow to cool. Thaw and slice shrimp in half lengthwise. Combine with rice, clams, chicken, celery, peas, green pepper and onions. Blend mayonnaise with remaining ingredients. Pour over shrimp mixture and toss lightly. Chill. Use sliced tomatoes for garnish, or toss with salad.

Yield: 6–8 servings

HOW TO FEED A CROWD SALAD

- **2 pounds cooked and cubed ham**
- **2 pounds cooked and chopped chicken**
- **2 pounds grated Cheddar cheese**
- **2 pounds cooked and crumbled bacon**
- **1 dozen grated hard boiled eggs**
- **4 peeled and diced avocados**
- **1 pound sliced fresh mushrooms**
- **1 large can sliced pitted ripe olives**
- **2 bunches chopped green onions**
- **2 bunches sliced radishes**
- **2 pints cherry tomatoes**
- **4 to 6 heads of lettuce, cut or torn in bite size pieces (use a variety of lettuce)**

Assign ingredients to participants. Put into a VERY VERY LARGE CONTAINER to toss. Use favorite dressing or set out a variety of dressings. Serve with fresh bread.

Yield: 20 servings

Note: This is a fun meal to prepare together. We usually followed this with a deep dish peach cobbler for dessert.

TOMATO–BASIL VINAIGRETTE

4 large sliced tomatoes
¼ cup plus 2 tablespoons chopped fresh basil

SAUCE:
¼ cup plus 2 tablespoons olive oil
2 tablespoons vinegar
½ teaspoon salt
⅛ teaspoon pepper

Place tomatoes in 9x13 inch dish. Sprinkle with fresh basil. Combine sauce in a jar. Cover and shake. Pour sauce over tomatoes and basil. Chill for 3 hours.

Yield: 6–8 servings

HONEY MUSTARD DRESSING

2 gallons mayonnaise
5 cups vegetable oil
5 cups mustard
5 cups honey
1½ cups cider vinegar
⅛ cup onion salt
1 tablespoon cayenne pepper

Mix ingredients and pour into individual jars.

Yield: 12 quarts

POPPY SEED DRESSING

1½ cups white sugar
2 teaspoons dry mustard
2 teaspoons salt
⅔ cup white vinegar
3 tablespoons onion juice
2 cups salad oil (NEVER use olive oil)
3 tablespoons poppy seeds

Mix first 5 ingredients and slowly add oil, beating constantly. Add poppy seeds and beat a few minutes until mixed.

Yield: 2 pints

Note: Store in refrigerator. Use an electric mixer to mix or blender set on medium speed.

RED WINE VINAIGRETTE

- 1 cup oil
- ½ cup red wine vinegar
- ½ cup sugar
- ½ teaspoon onion salt
- ½ teaspoon dry mustard
- 1 teaspoon dried onions
- 2 tablespoons poppy seeds
- 1½ teaspoons grated grapefruit peel
- ¼ cup grapefruit juice

Mix all ingredients together in a jar and pour over fruited Spinach Salad or Salad La Parisienne Salad.

Yield: 5 cups

Pansies, nasturtiums, bachelor's buttons and snapdragons can be used as edible garnishes.

CRANBERRY CUMBERLAND SAUCE

- 1 cup whole cranberry sauce
- 2 tablespoons lemon juice
- ¼ cup red wine
- 1 orange rind
- 1 teaspoon paprika
- ½ teaspoon ground ginger
- ½ teaspoon dry mustard
- 3 tablespoons sugar

Combine all ingredients in a pan, cook over low heat until jelly and sugar melt.

Yield: 1½ cups

Breads

BUTTONS & BOWS BREAKFAST BISCUITS

- 2 cups flour
- 2 tablespoons sugar
- 2 teaspoons baking powder
- 1 teaspoon nutmeg
- ½ teaspoon salt
- ¼ teaspoon cinnamon
- ⅓ cup shortening
- ¾ cup buttermilk
- ¼ cup melted butter or margarine
- ½ cup sugar

Preheat oven to 425 degrees. Measure flour, sugar, baking powder, nutmeg, salt and cinnamon into bowl, cut in shortening, stir in buttermilk until soft dough forms. Knead 15-20 times on lightly floured surface. Roll ½ inch thick. Cut with donut cutter. Twist outside ring to make bow (figure 8). Place buttons and bows on ungreased baking sheet. Bake 10 minutes or until light brown. Dip hot biscuits in melted butter, then in sugar. Serve warm.

Yield: 1½ dozen

CHEESE BISCUITS

- 2 cups buttermilk pancake mix
- ¾ cup shredded Cheddar cheese
- ⅔ cup milk

Combine ingredients. Beat vigorously 30 seconds. Drop dough on ungreased baking sheet. Bake at 450 degrees for 8-10 minutes. Brush tops with melted butter.

Yield: 12 biscuits

MAKE AHEAD RAISIN BRAN MUFFINS

- 1 15-ounce box raisin bran cereal
- 5 cups flour
- 3 cups sugar
- 5 teaspoons soda
- 2 teaspoons salt
- 4 beaten eggs
- 1 quart buttermilk
- 1 cup corn oil

Combine first 5 ingredients in a very large bowl. Mix, make a well in center of mixture, add eggs, buttermilk and oil. Stir just enough to moisten ingredients. Cover and store in refrigerator until ready to bake. Batter can be kept in refrigerator as long as 6 weeks. When ready to bake, spoon batter into greased muffin pans filling ⅔ full. Bake 400 degrees for 15 minutes.

Yield: 48 muffins

PECAN-RAISIN MUFFINS

1¾ cups flour
¼ cup sugar
1 tablespoon baking powder
⅓ cup margarine
½ cup chopped pecans
⅓ cup raisins
1 egg
¾ cup milk

Mix flour, sugar and baking powder. Add margarine, mix until coarse. Mix in pecans and raisins. Beat together egg and milk. Add to mixture slowly. Fill 12 greased muffin cups about ¾ full. Bake 15-20 minutes at 400 degrees. For breakfast you can add ½ cup grated Cheddar cheese and ⅓ cup crumbled bacon to mixture.

Yield: 12 muffins

BERRY GOOD MUFFINS

½ cup milk
¼ cup vegetable oil
1 egg
1½ cups flour
½ cup sugar
2 teaspoons baking powder
½ teaspoon salt
1 cup berries (raspberries, blueberries or strawberries—If using strawberries, cut in quarters)

Preheat oven to 400 degrees. Stir together milk, oil and eggs. Sift together dry ingredients and add to milk stirring only until moistened. Fold in berries quickly. Fill greased muffin pans ½ full. Sprinkle top with cinnamon and sugar mixture. Bake 20-25 minutes.

Yield: 12 muffins

BLUEBERRY FEATHER MUFFINS

⅓ cup sugar
¼ cup butter
1 egg
2⅓ cups sifted flour
½ teaspoon salt
4 teaspoons baking powder
1 cup milk
1½ cups rinsed and drained blueberries
1 teaspoon vanilla

TOPPING:
½ cup sugar
½ teaspoon cinnamon
⅓ cup flour
¼ cup butter

Beat sugar, butter and egg until fluffy. Sift flour, salt and baking powder together and add mixture alternating with milk. Add vanilla. Fold in berries. Spoon into large greased muffin pans (¾ full). Add topping that is mixed together. Bake 375 degrees for 20-25 minutes.

Yield: 1½ dozen

RASPBERRY STREUSEL MUFFINS

- **1½ cups unbleached all purpose flour**
- **¼ cup granulated sugar**
- **¼ cup packed dark brown sugar**
- **2 teaspoons baking powder**
- **¼ teaspoon salt**
- **1 teaspoon ground cinnamon**
- **1 lightly beaten egg**
- **½ cup melted unsalted butter**
- **½ cup milk**
- **1¼ cups fresh raspberries**
- **1 teaspoon grated lemon zest**

STREUSEL TOPPING:

- **½ cup chopped pecans**
- **½ cup packed dark brown sugar**
- **¼ cup unbleached all purpose flour**
- **1 teaspoon ground cinnamon**
- **2 tablespoons unsalted butter, melted**
- **1 teaspoon grated lemon zest**

GLAZE:

- **½ cup confectioner's sugar**
- **1 tablespoon fresh lemon juice**

Preheat oven to 350 degrees. Line muffin cups with paper liners. To make the muffin batter, sift the flour, granulated sugar, brown sugar, baking powder, salt and cinnamon together into medium-size mixing bowl and make a well in the center. Place the egg, melted butter, and milk in the well. Stir with wooden spoon just until ingredients are combined. Quickly stir in the raspberries and lemon zest. Fill each muffin cup ¾ full with the batter. To make streusel topping, combine all ingredients and sprinkle this mixture evenly over the top of each muffin. Bake 20 to 25 minutes or until nicely browned and firm. Mix the glaze mixture together and drizzle over the warm muffins with a spoon. Serve warm.

Yield: 16 muffins

MINI APPLE MUFFINS

- **2 cups granulated sugar**
- **2 eggs**
- **½ cup oil**
- **1½ teaspoons vanilla**
- **2 teaspoons lemon juice**
- **2 cups flour**
- **2 teaspoons baking soda**
- **2 teaspoons cinnamon**
- **4 cups chopped apples**
- **1 cup chopped nuts**

Mix all ingredients together. Prepare mini muffin pans with vegetable spray or line with paper cups. Bake at 350 degrees for 10-12 minutes.

Yield: 50 mini muffins

VEGGIE APPLE MUFFINS

- **2 cups all purpose flour**
- **2 cups shredded carrots**
- **1 cup shredded zucchini**
- **1 chopped Granny Smith apple**
- **1¼ cups granulated sugar**
- **¾ cup golden raisins**
- **¾ cup shredded coconut**
- **½ cup coarsely chopped almonds**
- **1 tablespoon cinnamon**
- **2 teaspoons baking soda**
- **1¼ teaspoons grated orange peel**
- **1 teaspoon vanilla extract**
- **½ teaspoon salt**
- **3 large eggs**
- **1 cup vegetable oil**

Preheat oven to 375 degrees. Grease muffin cups. Mix all ingredients except eggs and oil in large bowl. Beat eggs and oil in another bowl to blend. Stir into flour, zucchini, carrots, apple mixture. Spoon into each cup, filling only ⅔ full. Bake until tester inserted in centers comes out clean, about 25 minutes.

Yield: 24 muffins

ZUCCHINI MUFFINS

- **3 eggs**
- **1 cup olive oil**
- **1 cup granulated sugar**
- **1 cup packed brown sugar**
- **1 tablespoon maple flavoring**
- **2 cups shredded zucchini**
- **2½ cups flour**
- **½ teaspoon baking powder**
- **2 teaspoon salt**
- **2 teaspoon baking soda**
- **½ cup wheat germ**
- **1 cup chopped walnuts**
- **sesame seeds to sprinkle on top**

In large bowl mix eggs, oil, sugars, and maple flavoring. Beat until thick, foamy and light in color. In separate bowl sift flour, baking powder, salt, soda, wheat germ and walnuts. Add dry mixture to egg mixture and gently stir. Spray muffin pans with vegetable spray (best to spray with olive oil). Fill the pans ½ full and sprinkle sesame seeds on top. Bake at 350 degrees for 20 to 25 minutes.

Yield: 75 mini-muffins or 25 regular size muffins

Daylilies and hibiscus are edible, but the pistols and stamens which contain pollen should be removed or they will affect the flavor.

HEAVENLY LIGHT ROLLS

1 cup yellow cornmeal
2½ cups cold water
½ cup butter
2 packages dry yeast
⅓ cup water (110 degrees)
1 cup milk
1 cup sugar
2 teaspoons salt
7½ cups flour
2 eggs

Boil first 2 ingredients until thick, add ½ cup butter. Dissolve yeast in ⅓ cup water. Let stand 5 minutes. Scald 1 cup milk - cool to lukewarm. Mix milk, yeast, sugar, salt, eggs, then add cornmeal to mixture. Mix until smooth. Gradually add flour until you can handle dough. Knead on a floured board until smooth. Place in greased bowl. Brush with melted butter. Cover with damp warm cloth until double. Punch down, let rise again until double. Pull off, shape into small rolls. Place on greased baking sheet. Let rise again until double. Bake 375 to 400 degrees, 15 to 20 minutes.

Yield: 60 medium size rolls

RUBY'S ROLLS

2 cups milk
¼ cup shortening
5-6 cups flour
½ cup warm water
2 packages dry yeast
1 tablespoon sugar
¼ cup honey
1 egg
1½ teaspoons salt

Heat milk to scalding, add shortening, stir until melted. Let cool to lukewarm. Add 1 cup flour, stir until smooth. Add yeast and sugar to water, let dissolve. Add milk and flour mixture, add honey, salt and egg. Stir in 2 more cups of flour, beat well, add 2 more cups of flour and stir to make not sticky. Knead 5-10 minutes adding more flour if necessary. Let rise until double or put in refrigerator to rise for next day. With this dough you can make rolls, bread, cinnamon or sticky buns. To make cinnamon rolls, roll out half of dough, about 12x12. Spread with melted butter, mix ½ cup sugar and 1 teaspoon cinnamon, sprinkle on top. Can add ½ cup raisins. Let rise until double. Bake 30 minutes in a 9x13 pan. For cloverleaf rolls, form into shapes of balls. Put into muffins pans, let rise double. Bake 15 minutes at 375 degrees.

Yield: 1 dozen

90 MINUTE DINNER ROLLS

2 cups + 3 tablespoons unsifted flour
2 tablespoons granulated sugar
½ teaspoon salt
1 package active dry yeast
½ cup milk
¼ cup water
2 tablespoons margarine

Mix ¾ cup flour, sugar, salt and undissolved yeast. Heat milk, water and margarine to almost boiling. Gradually add to the above dry ingredients and beat 2 minutes at medium speed. Add ¼ cup more flour and beat at high speed for another 2 minutes. (A whisk could be used). Add enough flour to mix to make a soft dough. On floured board knead for 2 to 3 minutes. Divide dough into 12 equal parts and shape into balls. Place in greased round 8 inch pan. Place a 2 inch depth of boiling water in large pan on low rack of oven. Set oven to lowest heat. Set covered rolls on rack above pan of water. Close oven door and let rise 30 to 35 minutes. Uncover rolls, remove water pan. Bake at 375 degrees for 25 to 30 minutes or until slightly brown. Remove from oven and rub tops with butter. Serve warm or reheat in microwave for 35 seconds.

Yield: 12 rolls

CRANBERRY BREAD

2½ cups cranberries
2½ cups granulated sugar
3¾ teaspoons baking powder
5 tablespoons melted shortening
1¼ teaspoons soda
1½ cups nuts
3 eggs
3 oranges

Mix first 7 ingredients. Juice and grate the rind from oranges. Add enough water to juice to make 1¾ cups plus 2 tablespoons and add to batter. Distribute batter between 4 coffee cans or 3 loaf pans. Bake 350 degrees for 50 or 60 minutes.

Yield: 4 loaves

BEER BREAD

3 cups self-raising flour
3 tablespoons granulated sugar
1 12-ounce can beer
½ cup melted butter

Mix all above ingredients. Bake at 350 degrees for 45 minutes. Put melted butter on top of bread and bake another 15 minutes.

Yield: 1 loaf

HOMEMADE BREAD

- **2 1-pound coffee cans**
- **4 cups unsifted flour**
- **1 package dry yeast**
- **½ cup water**
- **½ cup milk**
- **½ cup butter or margarine**
- **¼ cup sugar**
- **1 teaspoon salt**
- **2 beaten eggs**

Mix 2 cups flour with yeast. Put water, milk, butter, sugar and salt in small saucepan over low heat. Stir occasionally until butter melts. Cool 5 minutes. Add liquids to flour and yeast, alternately add eggs and additional flour. Mix well. Knead by hand until stiff. Place ½ the dough mixture in each can and allow to rise until 1 inch from the top. Bake at 375 degrees for about 35 minutes.

Yield: 2 cans

POPPY SEED BREAD

- **2 cups sugar**
- **1½ cups vegetable oil**
- **4 eggs**
- **1 teaspoon vanilla**
- **3 cups flour**
- **1½ teaspoons soda**
- **1 13-ounce can evaporated milk**
- **¼ cup poppy seeds**
- **1½ cups chopped nuts**
- **⅛ teaspoon salt**

Mix first 4 ingredients together. Then add the rest of the ingredients and beat together. Put in loaf pans and bake at 350 degrees for 1 hour.

Yield: 2 loaves

CORN OR EGG BREAD

- **1½ cups cornmeal**
- **3 tablespoons enriched flour**
- **1 teaspoon salt**
- **1 teaspoon soda**
- **2 cups buttermilk**
- **1 egg**
- **2 tablespoons melted shortening**

Mix dry ingredients, add buttermilk and egg. Melt shortening in a heavy cast iron skillet. Pour the hot shortening into batter, mix. Pour into the hot iron skillet and bake at 450 degrees for 20 to 25 minutes or until golden brown.

Yield: 1 loaf

IT DOESN'T GET ANY BETTER THAN THIS CORNBREAD

1 cup self-rising cornmeal
2 eggs
1 8¾-ounce can cream style corn
½ cup salad oil
1 cup sour cream
salt to taste

Combine all ingredients, mixing well. Pour into greased 9 inch pan. Bake at 400 degrees for 20-30 minutes.

Yield: 8 pieces

TEXAS STYLE CORNBREAD

2 cups self-rising cornmeal
¼ teaspoon baking soda
1 10¾-ounce can undiluted golden corn soup or 18½-ounce can cream style corn + 2 ounces of milk
1 cup buttermilk
2 eggs
⅓ cup vegetable oil
1 4.5-ounce chopped green chilies
1½ cups shredded Cheddar cheese

Combine soup, buttermilk, eggs, vegetable oil, green chilies and Cheddar cheese. Mix soda with cornmeal and blend into soup mixture.

For corn sticks: Heat cast iron corn stick pan in hot oven for a few minutes. Remove pan from oven and spray with vegetable cooking spray. Spoon batter into hot pan and bake at 425 degrees for 15 minutes or until golden brown.

Yield: 2 dozen corn sticks

FOOD PROCESSOR ITALIAN BREAD

4½ cups flour (bread flour is best)
2 packages yeast
1 tablespoon granulated sugar
1 tablespoon salt
1 tablespoon butter

In processor put 1½ cups flour, yeast, sugar, salt and butter. Slowly add 1¾ cups warm water. Process 30 seconds. Add ¾ cup flour, process 30 seconds. Add 2 more cups (heaping) flour, Process 25 turns, if dough is too sticky, add more flour, 1 tablespoon at a time. Remove from processor, it shouldn't stick to your fingers. Cover with plastic wrap and let rest 20 minutes.

Divide into 2 pieces. Roll each piece into a 10x15 inch rectangle and roll up. Put on baking sheet. Let rise in refrigerator 2 to 4 hours. Brush with egg white. Cut slits, bake at 350 degrees for 30 minutes.

Yield: 2 loaves

PERSIMMON BREAD

- ¼ cup plus 2 tablespoons butter or margarine
- 1 cup sugar
- 2 eggs
- 1 cup persimmon pulp
- 1 teaspoon baking soda
- 2 cups flour
- 1 teaspoon baking powder
- 1 teaspoon salt
- ½ teaspoon cinnamon
- ½ teaspoon cloves
- ½ teaspoon nutmeg
- 1 cup chopped nuts
- 1 cup chopped dates

Stir baking soda into persimmon pulp and let stand until soda is dissolved. Mix together flour, baking powder, salt, cinnamon, cloves and nutmeg. Cream sugar and butter. Add eggs one at a time, mixing well after each addition. Add persimmon mixture. Gradually add flour mixture and beat well. Add nuts and dates. Divide into 5½x8½ inch loaf pans that have been sprayed with cooking spray. Bake at 350 degrees for 55 to 60 minutes or until pick comes out clean.

Yield: 2 loaves

SPICE BREAD

- 2 eggs
- 1 cup brown sugar
- 2 cups white sugar
- 2 cups buttermilk
- 1 cup salad oil
- 4 cups flour
- 1 teaspoon nutmeg
- 1 teaspoon cloves
- 2 teaspoons cinnamon
- 1 teaspoon salt
- 2 teaspoons soda

Mix first 5 ingredients together. Sift together next 6 ingredients and add to mixture. Mix well and pour into greased 5½x8½ inch loaf pans. Bake 1 hour at 350 degrees.

Yield: 2 loaves

PUMPKIN BREAD

- 3 cups sugar
- 4 eggs
- 1 teaspoon baking powder
- 2 teaspoons soda
- 1½ teaspoons salt
- 1 teaspoon cloves
- 1 teaspoon nutmeg
- 1 teaspoon cinnamon
- 1 cup oil
- ⅔ cup water
- 3½ cups sifted flour
- 2 cups pumpkin

Mix all above ingredients. Put in loaf pans and bake at 350 degrees for 1 hour and 15 minutes.

Yield: 2 loaves

IRISH SODA BREAD

- **2½ cups all purpose flour**
- **1 teaspoon baking soda**
- **1 teaspoon baking powder**
- **½ teaspoon salt**
- **1 tablespoon granulated sugar**
- **½ cup butter or margarine**
- **½ cup seedless raisins (plumped)**
- **2 tablespoons caraway seeds**
- **¾ cup milk**
- **3 tablespoons apple cider vinegar**

Sift flour with next 4 ingredients. Cut in butter with pastry blender. Stir in raisins and caraway seeds. Mix together milk and vinegar. Make a well in middle of flour mixture; add liquid all at once, stirring vigorously with fork until dry ingredients are moistened. Turn out onto lightly floured board. Knead gently 8 to 10 times. Shape into round ball. Place in a greased 8 inch pie plate. Cut a cross from side to side and brush with a little glaze. Bake at 400 degrees for 15 minutes; lower temperature to 375 degrees and bake 30 additional minutes. Remove from pan and cool 1 hour on rack.

Yield: 1 loaf

SAUSAGE BREAD

- **1 cup raisins (optional)**
- **1 pound pork or turkey sausage**
- **1½ cups brown sugar**
- **2 eggs**
- **3 cups flour**
- **1 teaspoon ginger**
- **1 teaspoon pumpkin pie spice**
- **1 teaspoon baking soda**
- **1 cup cold coffee**
- **1 cup chopped nuts (optional)**

Simmer raisins in a little hot water 4 or 5 minutes. Drain well and set aside. Mix uncooked sausage and sugar until well blended. Add eggs, mix well. Sift together dry ingredients except soda. Stir soda into coffee. Add flour and coffee mixtures alternately. Stir in nuts and raisins. Pour into greased and floured tube pan. Bake at 350 degrees, 1½ hours. Keeps for weeks in refrigerator.

Yield: 1 pan

TEXAS PEACH NUT BREAD

- 2 cups all purpose flour
- 2 teaspoons baking powder
- ½ teaspoon ground nutmeg
- ⅔ teaspoon salt
- ⅔ cup butter or margarine
- 1½ cups sugar
- 2 eggs
- 4 tablespoons sour cream
- 1 cup peeled, mashed fresh peaches
- 1 cup chopped pecans

Grease a 9x5x3 inch loaf pan. In a small bowl, stir together flour, baking powder, nutmeg and salt. In a large mixing bowl, cream butter and sugar, add eggs and sour cream and beat until light (or 2 minutes). Stir in flour mixture alternately with peaches. Stir in pecans. Pour into prepared pan and bake at 350 degrees for 50-60 minutes or until cake tester comes out clean. Cool 10 minutes in pan. Remove to wire rack and cool completely.

Yield: 1 loaf

 *Mint leaves and rose petals can be candied and used as edible garnishes.*

CRANBERRY SCONES

- 2 cups flour
- 3 tablespoons brown sugar
- 2 teaspoons baking powder
- ½ teaspoon baking soda
- ¼ cup butter (room temperature)
- 1 8-ounce carton sour cream (can use light)
- 1 egg
- ½ cup dried cranberries

In large mixing bowl stir flour, brown sugar, baking powder, baking soda and ½ teaspoon salt. Cut in butter until mixture resembles coarse crumbs. Separate egg and stir together egg yolk and sour cream.. Pour boiling water over fruit, let stand 5 minutes. Drain well and add to flour mixture along with sour cream. Add to flour mixture and stir until combined., Turn dough onto lightly floured surface and knead 10 to 12 strokes. Pat into a 7 inch circle. Cut into 12 wedges. Arrange wedges on a baking sheet about 1 inch apart. Beat egg white slightly, brush on wedges, lightly sprinkle with white sugar. Bake 400 degrees oven for 15-20 minutes. Cool 10 minutes. Serve warm.

Yield: 1 dozen

Note: Equally delicious with raisins or cherries instead of cranberries.

A+ APRICOT BANANA BREAD

½ cup softened butter
1 cup granulated sugar
2 beaten eggs
1½ cups flour
1 teaspoon baking soda
1 teaspoon salt
1 cup very ripe mashed bananas
½ cup chopped dried apricots
½ cup sour cream
1 teaspoon vanilla
½ cup chopped walnuts or pecans

Preheat oven to 350 degrees. Butter 9x5x3 inch loaf pan. Cream butter and sugar, add eggs and beat until mixed. Sift flour, soda and salt. Add to butter mixture and blend. Add bananas, apricots, sour cream, vanilla, and walnuts; stir. Pour into prepared pan. Bake 1 hour.

Yield: 1 loaf

MINI WHEAT LOAVES

2 cups scalded milk
2 envelopes yeast
1 egg
2 tablespoons shortening
⅓ cup honey or ⅓ cup sugar
2 teaspoons salt
1 cup whole wheat flour
3 cups bread flour

Heat milk, add honey or sugar, shortening to warm milk. Let cool and add yeast. Add salt and beaten egg. Add flour a little at a time. Knead, adding flour if needed. Put in greased pan. Cover with cloth and let rise until doubled, about 2 hours. Then knead and shape into rolls or small loaves and let rise again until doubled. Bake at 350 degrees until brown, 15 to 20 minutes.

Yield: 1 loaf

HERBED BREAD STICKS (AKA) GERI'S BREAD STICKS

1 loaf white bread
½ cup butter or margarine
¼ teaspoon Beau Monde seasoning
¼ teaspoon Greek seasoning
¼ teaspoon dill weed
¼ teaspoon garlic cheese spread (jar)

Melt butter with seasonings. Spread on bread slices. Cut slices into 4 lengthwise pieces. Bake in oven at 250 degrees for 30 minutes to 60 minutes.

EGG TWIST BREAD

- **2 loaves egg twist bread**
- **1 cup melted butter**
- **1 teaspoon tarragon vinegar**
- **1 teaspoon rosemary**
- **1 teaspoon ground thyme**
- **2 finely chopped fresh green onions**
- **1 teaspoon garlic powder or to taste**

Put foil in a 10x15 inch pan, pull egg bread apart into small pieces (roll size) or leave bread altogether. Mix remaining ingredients and spoon butter mixture on top. You can make ahead so butter will soak into bread. Fold foil around bread and bake at 350 degrees for 15-20 minutes.

Yield: 2 loaves

ZUCCHINI MUNCHIES

- **3 cups thinly sliced zucchini (5 small)**
- **1 cup baking mix**
- **½ cup sliced green onions**
- **½ cup grated Parmesan cheese**
- **2 tablespoons parsley**
- **½ teaspoon salt**
- **½ teaspoon Italian seasoning**
- **¼ teaspoon garlic powder**
- **½ cup vegetable oil**
- **4 beaten eggs**
- **⅛ teaspoon hot sauce**

Mix all ingredients and pour into a greased 8x8 inch glass pan. Bake 350 degrees for 25 minutes or until top is golden brown.

Yield: 16 pieces

CRÊPES

- **1½ cups all purpose flour**
- **⅛ teaspoon salt**
- **1 egg**
- **1½ cups milk**
- **2 tablespoons vegetable oil**
- **⅛ teaspoon granulated sugar**
- **½ teaspoon parsley (optional)**

Place all ingredients in a blender. Mix on low, then on high. Let stand 15 minutes, then cook in crêpe pan. Fill crêpes with Heard's chicken salad and drizzle with apricot sauce.

Yield: 28 (5-inch) crêpes

Main Dishes

PECOS CASSEROLE

- 4 tablespoons butter
- 2 pounds lean ground beef
- 1 large chopped onion
- 1 green chopped pepper
- 1 6-ounce can sliced mushrooms
- 2 teaspoons chili powder
- ¼ cup Worcestershire sauce
- ½ cup picante sauce
- ½ teaspoon salt
- ½ teaspoon pepper
- 1 10¾-ounce can tomato soup
- 1 13¼-ounce can cream style corn
- 1 10¾-ounce can tomatoes (with green chilies if desired)
- 1 12-ounce package noodles, cooked

Melt butter in heavy skillet or Dutch oven. Add meat, onion, green pepper, mushrooms, Worcestershire sauce, chili powder, salt and pepper to taste. Cook until meat is brown. Add soup, corn and tomatoes. Simmer 30 minutes. Cook noodles according to package directions and add to mixture. Pour into a 3 quart casserole and let cool. Bake 1 hour in a preheated 325 degree oven. A topping of grated cheese makes this dish special.

Yield: 8–10 servings

Note: This can be placed in freezer and baked a day or two later.

MEXICAN BEEF

- 1 teaspoon oil
- ½ pound ground meat
- 2 tablespoons chopped onion
- 2 cloves minced garlic
- ½ teaspoon pepper
- 2 tablespoons chopped coriander
- 1 teaspoon Worcestershire sauce
- ½ teaspoon salt
- 3 medium zucchini squash
- 1 11-ounce can corn salsa

Sauté meat, garlic and pepper in oil until the meat is lightly brown. Add onions and continue cooking until they are translucent. Slice squash, cook until tender, drain and add with can of corn to the cooked meat. Serve in hot tortillas topped with salsa.

Yield: 6 servings

FIESTA FOR A CROWD

- **4 pounds ground meat, 90% lean**
- **3 chopped onions**
- **2 1-pound cans tomatoes**
- **1 16-ounce can tomato sauce**
- **1 16-ounce can of tomato purée or 2 small cans**
- **4 tablespoons chili powder**
- **2-3 tablespoons garlic salt**
- **1 30-ounce can ranch style beans**
- **1 large bag of Fritos**
- **1 24-ounce box instant rice, cooked**
- **1 pound sharp grated Cheddar cheese**
- **1 thinly sliced head lettuce**
- **2 diced tomatoes**
- **3 diced onions**
- **1 6-ounce can chopped black olives**
- **10 ounces chopped pecans**
- **7 ounces coconut**
- **picante sauce**

Cook meat and onions until brown. Drain grease off and add tomatoes, tomato sauce, tomato purée, garlic salt, and ranch style beans. Simmer for one hour. Add water if needed. Cook instant rice as directed on box and drain. Place remaining ingredients in separate bowls.

For serving: Crush Fritos and place a portion on each plate. Top with a serving of rice, meat sauce and the remaining ingredients in the order as listed.

Yield: 16–20 servings

GREEN CHILI CASSEROLE

- **¼ cup butter or margarine**
- **2 large finely chopped onions**
- **1 pound ground beef**
- **1 7-ounce can green chilies (or to taste)**
- **1 10¾-ounce can cream of mushroom soup**
- **½ cup water**
- **1 8-ounce can evaporated milk**
- **1 pound grated Cheddar cheese (or more to taste)**
- **tortilla chips or Fritos**

Sauté chopped onions in butter until tender. Add beef and cook until brown. Stir in chopped green chilies, soup, milk, and water; mix well. Line 8x12 inch baking dish with tortilla chips, layer with the grated cheese, meat mixture, repeating until all used. Top with crushed chips and grated cheese. Bake for 30 minutes at 375 degrees.

Yield: 8 servings

Note: May use chicken and cream of chicken soup.

SKILLET MEXICAN BEEF AND RICE

- **1 tablespoon olive oil**
- **1 cup rice**
- **1 pound of ground chuck**
- **1 medium finely chopped onion**
- **2 cloves of minced garlic**
- **1 15–ounce can of tomatoes**
- **4 bouillon cubes**
- **1 cup of warm water**
- **2 tablespoons of chili powder**
- **1 teaspoon salt**
- **cayenne pepper to taste**

Heat olive oil in covered skillet. Add rice and cook until the rice pops open (it will turn white). Stir constantly. Add the ground chuck and cook until brown. Add onion and garlic; cook until the onion becomes transparent. Add all other ingredients and mix thoroughly. Cover and simmer for 30 minutes. Stir from time to time. The liquid should be absorbed by the rice.

Yield: 6 servings

MAKE AHEAD BEEF ENCHILADAS

- **1 pound ground beef**
- **1 14.5–ounce can tomatoes**
- **1 6–ounce can tomato paste**
- **½ cup water**
- **½ cup chopped onion**
- **2 tablespoons chili powder**
- **1¼ teaspoons salt**
- **¼ teaspoon pepper**
- **1 8–ounce package corn tortillas**
- **oil**
- **2 cups shredded Cheddar cheese**

Brown meat, drain. Add tomatoes, tomato paste, water, onion and seasonings. Simmer 10 minutes. Fry tortillas in hot oil until softened and drain. Place rounded tablespoon of meat sauce and cheese on each tortilla and roll up tightly. Place seam side down in an 18x12 inch baking dish. Top with remaining sauce and cheese. Cover with aluminum foil and refrigerate overnight. Bake for 50 minutes at 375 degrees. If not refrigerated overnight, bake 20 minutes at 325 degrees.

Yield: 6–8 servings

SPANISH MEATLOAF

1 pound lean ground beef
½ cup chopped onion
½ cup soft bread crumbs
1 large slightly beaten egg
¼ cup chopped green pepper
¼ cup sliced olives with pimento
1 15-ounce can crushed tomatoes
1 teaspoon salt
¼ teaspoon black pepper
1 cup shredded Cheddar cheese

Mix chopped onion, bread crumbs, beaten egg, chopped green pepper, olives, salt and pepper with ¼ cup of the crushed tomatoes (reserve remainder for topping). Mold into a loaf and place in a 3 quart baking dish. Bake 45 minutes at 350 degrees. Add topping of ¼ cup crushed tomatoes mixed with 1 cup Cheddar cheese. Return to oven until cheese melts.

Yield: 4–6 servings

ELEGANT ROAST MEATLOAF

3 eggs
1½ teaspoons salt
¼ teaspoon pepper
¼ teaspoon thyme
¼ teaspoon nutmeg
cloves, pinch
¼ cup sour cream
1 cup soft bread crumbs
2 pounds of lean ground beef
2 tablespoons finely chopped onions
2 tablespoons chopped parsley
2 tablespoons chopped celery leaves
1 teaspoon chopped fresh chives
¼ teaspoon finely chopped garlic
6 slices bacon
barbecue sauce or ketchup

In a large bowl beat eggs with salt, pepper, thyme, nutmeg and cloves. Stir in sour cream and bread crumbs. Let stand until crumbs absorbs moisture. Add meat and vegetables. Mix well. With hands shape into a rounded loaf and place in an 8x11 inch baking dish. Tightly wrap with bacon strips, tucking bacon under the loaf. Bake 1 hour at 350 degrees. Brush generously with barbecue sauce or ketchup and bake another 20 to 30 minutes.

Yield: 8–10 servings

MEATLOAF FLORENTINE WITH MUSHROOM SAUCE

1 egg, slightly beaten
1½ cups fresh bread crumbs
1 cup milk
2 tablespoons soy sauce
1 tablespoon pepper sauce
½ cup finely chopped onion
1 pound ground chuck
1 pound sausage (regular)
2 10-ounce packages frozen chopped spinach

Combine all ingredients except spinach. On a sheet of heavy duty aluminum foil or butcher paper, pat mixture into a rectangle about 7x10 and 1 inch thick. Squeeze thawed spinach until dry and spread over top. Using the foil or paper, roll the mixture up like a jelly roll. Remove foil or paper. Seal the ends of the meat loaf and place in a 9x13 inch baking dish. Bake for approximately 1½ hours at 350 degrees.

MUSHROOM SAUCE:
1 15-ounce can beef broth
1 2½-ounce jar drained sliced mushrooms
2-3 tablespoons cornstarch
1-2 tablespoon cool water
salt and pepper to taste

Heat beef broth in small saucepan and add mushrooms. Whisk the cornstarch in a small amount of water; add to sauce a little at a time until desired thickness is reached. Adjust taste with salt and pepper or beef bouillon if necessary. Serve over hot meatloaf.

Yield: 8 servings

BUSY DAY MEATLOAF

1 pound ground turkey
1 pound lean ground beef
1 15.25-ounce can Hunt's Meatloaf Fixin's
¾ cup seasoned or plain bread crumbs
½ cup chopped green pepper
½ cup chopped red pepper (optional)
1 medium chopped onion
2 eggs
1 teaspoon salt or to taste
½ teaspoon pepper or to taste

Mix ground turkey, ground beef, 1 cup Meatloaf Fixin's (reserve remainder), ¾ cup bread crumbs, chopped green and red peppers, chopped onion and egg. Add salt and pepper. Shape into loaf and bake in 3 quart baking dish at 350 degrees for one hour.

Heat remainder of Meatloaf Fixin's Sauce and serve over meatloaf.

Yield: 8-10 servings

MEATLOAF WITH SAUCE MONTARDE

- **2 tablespoons butter**
- **1 cup chopped onion**
- **1 peeled and diced tart apple**
- **1 teaspoon curry powder**
- **2 pounds lean ground sirloin**
- **½ cup dry bread crumbs**
- **1 egg**
- **½ cup milk (scant)**
- **2 tablespoons sugar**
- **1½ teaspoons salt**
- **¼ teaspoon pepper**
- **½ cup sliced and toasted almonds**

Sauté onion and apple in butter over medium heat about 10 minutes. Stir in curry; cook 1 minute and turn into bowl. To the ground sirloin add crumbs, egg, milk, sugar, salt, pepper and almonds. Mix well. Form into loaf and place in an 8x12 inch baking dish. Bake 1 hour at 350 degrees. Serve with Montarde Sauce.

MONTARDE SAUCE:

- **½ cup whipping cream**
- **½ cup chicken broth**
- **2 tablespoons butter**
- **2 tablespoons flour**
- **2 tablespoons Dijon mustard**
- **1 raw egg yolk**
- **1 teaspoon dry Vermouth**
- **¼ teaspoon salt**
- **¼ teaspoon white pepper**

Microwave whipping cream and broth on high for 1 minute in a large glass measuring cup. Blend in remaining ingredients and microwave for 2 minutes on high. Whisk briskly, and microwave on high 1 more minute. Let stand 5 minutes. Serve hot or warm.

Yield: 6 servings

 *The opossum is the only marsupial (pouched animal) found in North America.*

FILLET OF BEEF CHAUCER

- **8 fillet mignon steaks, 1 inch thick (6 to 8–ounces)**
- **1 crushed clove garlic**
- **1½ teaspoons seasoning salt**
- **¼ teaspoon seasoning pepper**
- **5 tablespoons butter (no substitute)**
- **2 tablespoons brandy**
- **3 tablespoons flour**
- **2 teaspoons tomato paste**
- **1 teaspoon crushed garlic**
- **¾ cup red wine**
- **1 cup chicken broth**
- **½ cup beef broth**
- **½ teaspoon Worcestershire sauce**
- **2 tablespoons currant jelly**
- **½ pound fresh sliced mushrooms**

Place steaks on work surface in a single layer. In a small bowl make paste with clove of garlic, salt, pepper and rub into both sides of steak. Heat 1 tablespoon butter in a large heavy skillet (not non–stick) until very hot. Sauté 4 steaks at a time until brown on both sides but still raw in middle. Put steaks in a 9x13 inch casserole. Add brandy to skillet and cook over moderate heat stirring constantly to scrape up brown bits. Add ½ stick butter. When melted and foamy, stir in flour. Reduce heat to low and cook until mixture is golden. Stir in tomato paste and garlic; mixture will look grainy. Remove pan from heat and whisk in wine, chicken and beef broth. Return to heat bringing to a boil, stirring constantly. Reduce heat to simmer and cook 10 minutes. Stir in Worcestershire and jelly. When jelly melts stir in mushrooms. Sauce should be coating consistency. If too thick add more wine. Cool. Pour over steaks. Can be refrigerated over night. Preheat oven 400 degrees and bake uncovered 15 to 20 minutes for medium rare or 20 to 25 for medium done. Spoon sauce over steaks when serving.

Yield: 8 servings

Note: If refrigerated over night bring to room temperature before cooking.

NO PEEK CASSEROLE

- **2 pounds stew meat (chuck roast cut into 1½ inch pieces)**
- **1 10¾–ounce can onion soup**
- **1 10¾–ounce can cream of celery soup**
- **1 10¾–ounce can cream of mushroom soup**

Mix all together in a large heavy covered pot. Cook covered 8 hours in a preheated 250 degree oven. No seasoning and no liquid. Do not peek. Serve over rice or pasta.

Yield: 4–6 servings

BEEF TENDER WITH MUSTARD–HORSERADISH CREAM

1 beef tenderloin, 5 to 7 pounds, trimmed
3 tablespoons olive oil
1 tablespoon garlic powder
1 tablespoon seasoned salt
½ cup liquid smoke
cracked pepper
¼ cup melted margarine

Rub beef with oil, then rub in garlic powder and seasoned salt. Pour liquid smoke evenly over top and finish with a grind of pepper. Cover and refrigerate for at least 12 hours. Preheat oven to 375 degrees. Remove beef from marinade and place in roasting pan. If desired pour melted margarine over beef tenderloin. Roast uncovered for 40 minutes, or until a meat thermometer inserted at thickest point of meat registers 140 degrees. (For 2 tenders, increase time to 50 minutes.) Turn the meat once while cooking. Remove from oven and allow to stand about 10 minutes. Cut into slices. Serve with Mustard–Horseradish Cream.

MUSTARD–HORSERADISH CREAM:
1 cup cream
¼ cup mustard
¼ cup bottled white horseradish
juice of ½ lemon

In a small bowl whip cream until stiff. Fold in mustard, horseradish and lemon juice. Refrigerate until serving time.

Yield: 8–10 servings

BRISKET

4–6 pounds brisket
1 4-ounce bottle liquid smoke
1 teaspoon onion salt
1 teaspoon garlic salt
1 teaspoon celery salt
1 cup Worcestershire sauce
2–3 cups barbecue sauce

Place brisket in a 9x13 inch foil lined baking dish and sprinkle bottle of liquid smoke over each side. Mix onion, garlic and celery salts; rub on each side of brisket. Cover brisket with foil and seal tightly. Let sit in refrigerator overnight. Next day, pour off juice. Sprinkle with Worcestershire sauce. Seal with foil (air tight) and cook in a preheated 275 degree oven for 4 to 5 hours. Pour barbecue sauce over brisket and cook another hour until tender.

Yield: 8–10 servings

ITALIAN BEEF BRISKET

5–6 pound brisket
1 tablespoon Accent
1 tablespoon garlic salt
1 teaspoon seasoning salt
½ cup Italian salad dressing
1 1.5–ounce package of beef brown gravy mix
1 2–ounce package of dry onion soup mix
1 3–ounce can sliced mushrooms

Line a large roasting pan with heavy aluminum foil and place the brisket on it. Mix Accent, garlic salt and seasoning salt; rub on all sides of the brisket. Mix the next four ingredients and pour over the top. Fold the foil over the brisket to seal tightly. Bake in a 300 degree oven, 1 hour per pound. Leftovers may be frozen for later use.

Yield: 8 servings

LASAGNA

1 pound Italian sausage or ground beef
1 tablespoon minced garlic
1 teaspoon dried basil
1 teaspoon dried oregano
1½ teaspoons salt
1 pound can tomatoes (2 cups)
2 6–ounce cans tomato paste
1 10–ounce package of lasagna noodles
3 cups fresh ricotta cheese or cottage cheese
½ cup grated Parmesan cheese
2 tablespoons parsley flakes
2 beaten eggs
1 teaspoon salt
½ teaspoon pepper
1 pound thinly sliced mozzarella cheese

Brown meat slowly and drain well. Add next five ingredients. Simmer for 30 minutes uncovered. Cook noodles and drain. Combine remaining ingredients except mozzarella cheese. Place half of the noodles in a 9x13 inch baking dish and spread with ½ of cheese mixture, ½ mozzarella and ½ meat sauce. Repeat layers. Bake 30 minutes at 375 degrees. Before serving, top with more grated Parmesan and (or) mozzarella and heat until cheese melts.

Yield: 8 servings

Note: Can be made a day ahead using uncooked noodles.

CHICKEN FRIED STEAK

2 slices tenderized round steak ¾ inches thick
2 eggs
1½ cups milk
2 cups flour
½ teaspoon baking powder
½ teaspoon salt
¼ teaspoon pepper

Trim any fat from steak and cut into 8 pieces. Beat eggs and milk. Mix baking powder, salt and pepper with flour. Dip steak into egg and milk mixture and dredge in flour. Redip and redredge in the flour mixture. Heat shortening in heavy skillet to level ¼ inch (or enough that the bottom and sides of steak are covered). Cook on high until meat is brown on both sides. Place on platter and keep warm. Serve with cream gravy.

CREAM GRAVY:
¼ cup drippings from skillet
4 tablespoons flour
2 cups milk

Pour the grease out of skillet, leaving only ¼ cup of drippings. Stir in 4 tablespoons flour and make a roux (flour will be browned). Gradually add 2 cups milk, stirring until slightly thickened. Salt and pepper to taste.

Yield: 4 servings

 *Hummingbirds can beat their wings 100 times per second.*

MARINATED FLANK STEAK

¼ cup soy sauce
3 tablespoons honey
2 tablespoons white vinegar
1½ teaspoons ground ginger
1½ teaspoons garlic powder
¾ cup salad oil
1 tablespoon minced onion
1½ pounds flank steak that has not been tenderized

Mix together soy sauce, honey and vinegar. Blend in ginger, garlic powder, minced onion and oil. Pour over steak. Refrigerate and let stand 4 hours or overnight. Turn meat occasionally. Cook over charcoal or gas grill, 8 to 10 minutes per side. Slice at an angle.

Yield: 4–6 servings

BARBECUE BEEF

- **6 pound pot roast**
- **2 pounds ground beef**
- **3 medium chopped onions**
- **1 large chopped stalk of celery**
- **2 tablespoons vinegar**
- **3 tablespoons brown sugar**
- **2 teaspoons chili powder**
- **Tabasco sauce to taste**
- **Worcestershire sauce (dash)**
- **1 42–ounce jar mild barbecue sauce, not hickory**

Place the meat in a large roasting pan. Lightly brown the ground beef with the chopped onions. Add the chopped celery, vinegar, brown sugar, chili powder, Tabasco and Worcestershire making a sauce. Pour over the pot roast. Add enough water so the meat is covered. Bake 7 or 8 hours at 325 degrees. Cool and pour off the grease. Fork or pull apart with hands and add one bottle of smoky barbecue sauce. Heat and serve.

Yield: 20 servings or 40 on small biscuit size buns

SWEET AND SALTY BAR–B–QUE BEEF

- **6 pound eye of round**
- **½ cup Worcestershire sauce**
- **4 ounces Scotch or Bourbon**
- **2 cloves minced garlic**
- **4 teaspoons granulated sugar**
- **1 teaspoon ground black pepper**
- **¼ teaspoon ground ginger**
- **½ cup salt**
- **½ cup sugar**

Mix Worcestershire sauce, Scotch or Bourbon, garlic, sugar, pepper and ginger in a bowl large enough to marinate the round; soak over night in the refrigerator, turning frequently. Combine the remaining salt and sugar on a flat plate. Remove meat from the marinade and dry with paper towels before coating with salt and sugar mix. Discard any salt mixture which does not adhere readily. Cover and grill over a low charcoal fire until charred on the outside and juicy on the inside. 40 minutes for rare meat. Serve in very thin slices with the meat juice on the side.

Yield: 10–12 servings

Note: A charbono is suggested.

TENDERLOIN OF BEEF WITH SAUCE DIANE AND WILD RICE

4 pounds tenderloin
2 cloves diced garlic
½ cup oil
½ cup lemon juice
½ cup red wine vinegar
¼ cup soy sauce
½ teaspoon Accent

Punch holes in tenderloin and place garlic clove pieces in them before cooking. Mix oil, lemon juice, vinegar, soy, Accent and pour over tenderloin. Preheat oven to 500 degrees. Bake tenderloin 30 minutes for medium doneness; baste during cooking. Use meat thermometer.

RICE:
1–2 packages of wild and brown rice
1 10¾ ounce can beef consommé (or chicken stock)
1 4–ounce can sliced water chestnuts
1 2.5–ounce jar of sliced mushrooms

Cook rice as directed on the package using undiluted beef consommé or chicken stock. Add 1 can sliced water chestnuts and the jar of sliced mushrooms. If the rice is cooked earlier, put it in a buttered baking dish and heat in microwave or oven just before serving.

SAUCE DIANE:
½ cup melted butter
¾ pound sliced fresh mushrooms
1½ cups sliced green onions, using part of green tops
2 teaspoons mustard
1 tablespoon lemon juice
1 tablespoon Worcestershire sauce
1 teaspoon salt
¼ cup chopped fresh parsley

Sauté green onions and mushrooms in melted butter for 5 minutes. Add remaining ingredients and cook an additional 5 minutes. Cut the tenderloin into thick slices and serve over rice. Pass Sauce Diane.

Yield: 8 servings

Swallows can make as many as 1,000 trips to get the mud required to build their nests.

MARINATED BEEF KABOB

3 pounds sirloin tip beef
¼ cup lemon juice
⅛ cup Worcestershire sauce
½ cup oil
½ cup soy sauce
⅛ cup prepared mustard (Ball Park)
2 cloves minced garlic
12 mushrooms
12 ½ to 1 inch chunks green peppers
12 cherry tomatoes
12 small onions

Trim all fat from sirloin tip and cut in 2 inch cubes. In a bowl large enough to hold the sirloin cubes, mix lemon juice, Worcestershire, oil, soy, mustard and garlic together. Marinate the meat for 8 to 12 hours in refrigerator. Turn occasionally. Remove the meat reserving the marinade. Place meat pieces on skewers alternating with mushroom, chunk of green pepper, tomato and small onion. Grill over medium hot coals 15 to 20 minutes basting with reserved marinade. Serve with rice.

Yield: 12 servings

BLACK BEAN SAUCE AND CHICKEN

4 skinless and boneless chicken breast halves
2 teaspoons ground cumin (divided for use)
1 teaspoon garlic salt
1 tablespoon vegetable oil
1 15–ounce rinsed and drained can black beans
1 8–ounce can drained whole kernel corn
⅔ cup picante sauce plus extra when served
½ cup chopped red or green bell pepper
2 tablespoons chopped cilantro

Sprinkle both sides of chicken with mix of garlic salt and 1 teaspoon of cumin. Heat oil in skillet over medium high heat. Cook chicken for 3 minutes. Turn chicken, reduce heat to medium. Mix beans, corn, picante sauce, bell pepper and remaining 1 teaspoon cumin with chicken mixture and spoon over chicken. Cook uncovered 6 to 7 minutes until chicken is tender. Move chicken to a warm platter and keep warm. Cook bean mixture 2 to 3 minutes more over high heat until thickened, stirring frequently. Spoon over the chicken. Sprinkle with cilantro. Serve with extra picante sauce.

Yield: 4 servings

GREEN CHICKEN ENCHILADAS

- **1½ cups finely chopped cooked chicken**
- **2½ cups fresh tomatillas or 1 18–ounce can tomatillas**
- **1 4–ounce can green chili peppers**
- **¼ cup chopped onions**
- **¼ cup cilantro leaves**
- **½ teaspoon sugar**
- **¼ teaspoon cumin**
- **½ to 1 cup reduced sodium chicken broth**
- **1 15¼–ounce can drained whole kernel corn**
- **⅓ cup light or regular cream cheese**
- **¼ cup fat free or light sour cream**
- **¼ cup sliced green onion**
- **8 8–inch flour tortillas**
- **¾ cup shredded reduced fat Monterey Jack cheese**

Rinse and seed the can of green chili peppers. Place tomatillas, peppers, onion, cilantro, sugar and cumin in a blender and add 1 cup of broth for fresh tomatillas or ½ cup for canned tomatillas. Secure top and blend until smooth. Transfer to saucepan and bring to a boil. Reduce heat and simmer uncovered for ten minutes. Combine chicken, corn, cream cheese, sour cream, onions. Spray 3 quart glass baking dish with non–stick cooking oil. Spray one side of each tortilla and place sprayed side down in large skillet over medium heat for 30 seconds. Remove and spoon ⅓ cup of filling onto each tortilla. Roll up and place, seam side down in a 9x13 inch baking dish. Pour the sauce over the rolled tortillas. Cover with foil. Bake for 30 minutes in a 350 degree oven. Top with cheese and bake uncovered for 3 minutes or until melted. Serve with salsa and more sour cream and cilantro if desired. Not only good, but heart healthy.

Yield: 8 servings

 *There are approximately 4,000 mammal species in the world.*

SOMBRERO CHICKEN TACOS

- **2 packages taco shells or 1 large bag tortilla chips**
- **6 boneless chicken breasts**
- **1 tablespoon oil**
- **1 teaspoon salt**
- **2 medium onions**
- **3 large cloves minced garlic**
- **2 1¼-ounce packages taco seasoning mix**
- **1 10-ounce can Ro-Tel tomatoes and green chilies**
- **1 10-ounce can of water**
- **1 4-ounce can of tomato paste**
- **¼ teaspoon salt**
- **¼ teaspoon pepper**
- **½ teaspoon ground cumin**

Slice breasts into small bite size pieces and salt. Sauté in hot oil until white. Chop onions, mince garlic and simmer until onions are slightly translucent, being careful not to brown or over cook. Add Ro-Tel tomatoes and green chilies, tomato paste, water and mix. Stir packages of taco seasoning mix into this mixture and let simmer for 30 to 40 minutes. Season to taste. This can be made ahead and frozen if desired. For a finer texture filling, place in blender and quickly pulse on shred for 1 minute.

DRESSING:

- **1 cup sour cream (lite is just as good)**
- **½ cup of Thick 'n & Chunky Salsa**

Combine and refrigerate until ready to serve.

SALAD LAYER:

- **1 head of lettuce**
- **1 medium red onion**
- **3 avocados**
- **4-6 sliced small tomatoes**
- **3 cups grated Cheddar cheese**

Shred lettuce, thinly slice onions and separate into rings. Peel avocados, pit and slice. In a large serving bowl layer shredded lettuce, sliced tomatoes, onion rings and avocados. Leave the center open for the bowl of warm taco filling. Top the layers with grated Cheddar cheese. Place the bowl of taco filling in the center. Spoon dressing around on top of the salad. Serve on a tray surrounded with warm taco shells or broken tortilla chips. Let each make their own tacos to their choice.

Yield: 12-16 servings

Porcupines can grow new quills to replace those that are lost.

CHICKEN AND BEAN BURRITOS

- **2 cups shredded cooked chicken**
- **1 15-ounce drained can pinto beans**
- **1 10¾-ounce can condensed cream of chicken soup**
- **1½ cups picante sauce**
- **½ cup sliced green onions with tops**
- **1 tablespoon chili powder**
- **1 teaspoon ground cumin**
- **12 7-inch flour tortillas**
- **1-2 cups shredded Monterey Jack or Cheddar cheese**

Combine chicken, beans, soup, ½ cup of picante sauce, onions, chili powder and cumin; mix well. Warm tortillas on grill. Spoon about ⅓ cup mixture down center of each tortilla. Roll up and place seam side down in lightly greased 9x13 inch baking dish. Spread with remaining 1 cup picante sauce. Cover dish tightly with foil. Bake at 350 degrees for 30 minutes. Sprinkle with cheese. Continue baking uncovered 3 minutes. Top as desired with additional picante sauce.

Yield: 6 servings

CHICKEN ENCHILADAS

- **1 3½ pound chicken**
- **1 large chopped onion**
- **1 large clove minced garlic**
- **½ cup margarine**
- **3 small cans green chilies and juice**
- **2 15½-ounce cans tomatoes with juice**
- **¾ teaspoon salt**
- **½ teaspoon pepper**
- **1 large bag of tortilla chips**
- **1½ pounds grated Cheddar cheese**
- **½ pint sour cream**
- **1 cup chicken broth**

Cook chicken until done; skin, debone and cut into bite size pieces. Brown onions and garlic in margarine until clear. Add chilies, tomatoes, salt and pepper; cook slowly for ½ hour. Add chopped chicken. Line a 9x13 inch casserole that has been buttered on the bottom with tortilla chips. Layer with ½ of chicken mixture and ½ of cheese. Repeat, but do not put chips on top of second layer. Pour 1 cup of chicken broth over layers and cover with ½ pint sour cream. Bake at 325 degrees for 30 to 45 minutes.

Yield: 16–18 servings

KING RANCH CHICKEN

- **8 chicken breast halves**
- **1 large diced onion**
- **1 10–ounce can chopped Ro–Tel tomatoes**
- **1 small package of soft flour tortillas, torn in small pieces**
- **½ pound grated longhorn cheese**
- **½ pound grated Monterey Jack cheese**
- **2 10¾–ounce cans cream of chicken soup**
- **1 4–ounce can chopped green chilies**
- **1 8–ounce carton sour cream**

Place chicken breasts on a foil lined pan, cover and cook for 20 minutes in a 350 degree oven. Cut into bite sized pieces. Lightly grease a 9x13 inch baking dish. Place the cubed chicken, onion and Ro–Tel tomatoes on the bottom. Tear tortillas into small pieces and place on top of chicken mixture. Sprinkle grated longhorn and Jack cheese on top. Mix soup, sour cream and green chilies and pour over the top. Bake at 350 degrees for 45 minutes.

Yield: 8 servings

Note: For low–fat cooking substitute Velveeta Light Cheese and Healthy Request soup. Omit sour cream if desired or use fat–free or lite sour cream.

RODEO DRIVE CHICKEN

- **2 cups finely chopped cooked chicken**
- **2 hard boiled eggs, finely chopped**
- **½ cup finely chopped ripe olives**
- **½ cup sliced toasted almonds**
- **1 teaspoon unflavored gelatin**
- **¼ cup cold water**
- **1 cup mayonnaise**
- **1 cup sour cream**
- **1 tablespoon grated onion**
- **½ teaspoon salt**
- **2 tablespoons lemon juice**
- **½ cup chopped fresh parsley**

Combine chicken with next three ingredients. Soak gelatin in cold water for 5 minutes and dissolve over hot water. Stir into mayonnaise. Add sour cream, onion, salt, lemon juice and parsley. Combine with chicken mixture. Pour into glass dish and chill until firm.

Yield: 6 servings

Note: This recipe must be doubled to make a 9x13 inch dish.

CHICKEN RAREBIT

- 1 broiler–fryer chicken
- 2 tablespoons butter
- ½ cup chopped green pepper
- ½ cup chopped onion
- ½ teaspoon salt
- ½ teaspoon pepper
- 1 cup evaporated milk or ½ cup evaporated milk with ½ cup stale beer
- 1 pound shredded extra sharp Cheddar cheese
- ½ teaspoon dry mustard
- 1 egg
- 1 teaspoon paprika
- 1 teaspoon Worcestershire sauce

Cook chicken, skin and debone. Chop into bite size pieces. Over medium heat, melt butter in large skillet. Sauté onions and pepper. Add chopped chicken, stirring until heated through. Add salt and pepper to taste. Remove to warm dish. Reduce burner heat to low and pour in milk (or ½ beer and ½ milk). Slowly stir cheese in mixture. In small bowl mix egg, mustard, paprika and Worcestershire sauce; slowly stir into cheese–milk mixture. Add chicken, chopped green pepper and onion. Continue to cook on low heat 5 minutes. Serve on toast points or over cooked rice.

Yield: 8–10 servings

 *A hedgehog has up to 7,000 spines.*

CHICKEN AND DRESSING CASSEROLE

- 1 chicken
- 2 cups chicken broth
- 2 10¾–ounce cans cream of chicken soup
- 1 8–ounce package cornbread stuffing mix
- ½ cup melted margarine

Boil chicken until done; remove skin and debone. Reserve 2 cups of the chicken broth. Cut the chicken into bite size pieces. Heat the chicken soup and stir in chicken broth. Add the cut up chicken to the soup broth mixture. Stir cornbread stuffing into melted margarine . Place one half of chicken mixture in an 8x12 inch baking dish and layer with one half of the stuffing, the remaining chicken soup mixture; ending with stuffing. Bake 45 minutes in a 350 degree oven.

Yield: 8 servings

CHICKEN PITA ROLLS

6 boneless and skinless chicken breast halves
4 tablespoons olive oil
½ lemon (squeeze for juice)
1 teaspoon oregano
1 teaspoon coarse black pepper
1 teaspoon salt
1 teaspoon parsley
1 16-ounce carton non fat yogurt
¼ teaspoon dill
2 cloves minced garlic
1 cucumber
6 pita rounds
1 large thinly sliced onion
1 large diced tomato
1 head of thinly sliced lettuce

Early in the day mix oil, lemon juice, oregano, pepper, parsley and salt in a container large enough to hold the chicken breasts. Marinate all day coating all sides. Early in the day peel and seed cucumber. Grate cucumber onto paper towel; press to remove as much liquid as possible. Mix cucumber with yogurt, pressed garlic, dill and salt to taste. Grill chicken. When ready to serve, slice à la fajita style. Place the thinly sliced head of lettuce and diced tomatoes on serving plate with a bowl of the garlic, cucumber, dill and yogurt. Warm and soften pita rounds. Serve like fajitas.

Yield: 6 servings

CHICKEN TENDER

1 cup rice
2 cups cooked and diced chicken
1 cup cream of chicken soup (undiluted)
¾ cup mayonnaise
1 cup diced celery
1 tablespoon lemon juice
1 4-ounce can mushrooms
1 teaspoon instant onion flakes or grated onion
1 teaspoon salt
½ cup slivered almonds
1 cup crushed cornflakes
1 tablespoon melted butter or margarine

Cook rice as directed on package. Mix with the next eight ingredients and turn into a lightly buttered 3 quart casserole. Mix cornflakes and almonds with melted butter and crumble over top. Bake at 375 degrees for 30 to 40 minutes.

Yield: 6–8 servings

EASY BAKED CHICKEN BREASTS

- **8 boneless and skinless chicken breasts**
- **8 slices Swiss cheese (4x4 inch)**
- **1 10¾-ounce can cream of chicken soup**
- **¼ cup dry white wine**
- **1 cup herb seasoned stuffing mix**
- **2–3 tablespoons butter or margarine**

Place breasts in lightly greased 8x12 inch baking dish. Top with cheese slices. Combine soup and wine, stir well. Pour sauce over the chicken. Crush herb seasoned stuffing mix and sprinkle over the chicken. Melt butter and drizzle over the crumb topping. Bake at 350 degrees for 45 minutes. Serve with rice.

Yield: 8 servings

Note: Especially nice with wild rice.

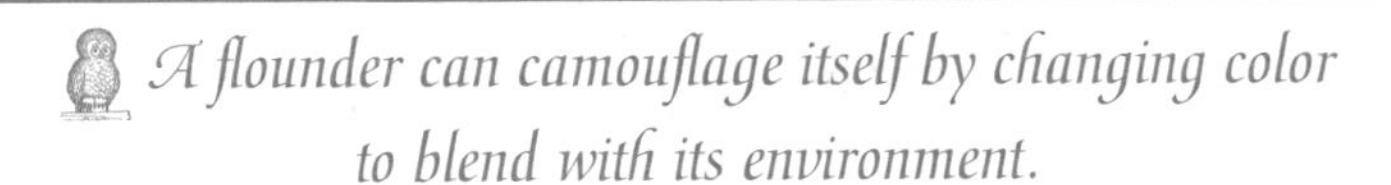

A flounder can camouflage itself by changing color to blend with its environment.

CHICKEN MARSALA

- **4 boneless–skinless chicken breast halves**
- **½ cup flour**
- **½ cup Parmesan cheese**
- **½ teaspoon garlic salt**
- **¼ cup butter or margarine**
- **2 cups chicken broth**
- **¼ teaspoon thyme**
- **½ cup Marsala**
- **1 pound of mushrooms**
- **1 small package of linguine noodles**

Cut chicken into bite size pieces and toss into plastic bag with flour and Parmesan cheese mixed with garlic salt to coat. Melt butter and sauté chicken. Remove chicken from pan. Stir broth, thyme and Marsala into butter, and continue to simmer. Meanwhile, in another pan sauté mushrooms in 2 tablespoons butter; add this to broth mixture along with the chicken. Simmer and serve over linguine noodles.

Yield: 4–6 servings

CHICKEN STIR FRY

- **6 tablespoons soy sauce**
- **4 tablespoons dry sherry**
- **2 tablespoons cornstarch**
- **4 cloves of minced garlic**
- **½ cup water**
- **2 tablespoons light olive oil**
- **2 boneless and skinless chicken breasts**
- **½ pound broccoli cut into small pieces**
- **1 small thinly sliced onion**
- **1 thinly sliced carrot**

Combine soy sauce, sherry, cornstarch, garlic and water; set aside. Place oil in a wok or large skillet; add chicken cut into bite size pieces and stir fry for 2 minutes or until done. Add vegetables and stir fry 4 minutes. Add soy sauce mixture. Stir and cook until slightly thickened. Serve over rice.

Yield: 4 servings

CRUNCHY CAPTAIN CHICKEN

- **2 tablespoons vegetable oil**
- **4 large boneless, skinless chicken breasts**
- **1 tablespoon curry powder**
- **1 15½-ounce can diced tomatoes**
- **1 teaspoon salt**
- **2 tablespoons chutney**
- **2 tablespoons currants**
- **1 cup chopped green peppers**
- **1 cup chopped red peppers**
- **1 medium chopped onion**
- **1 clove minced garlic**
- **¼ cup toasted slivered almonds**

In large skillet heat oil and brown chicken breasts. Remove from pan and add salt, curry powder, garlic, chopped onion and green and red peppers. Sauté until soft. Add tomatoes, chutney and currants. Return chicken to pan and simmer 20 to 30 minutes. To keep it juicy you may need to add ½ cup water. Serve over rice and garnish with toasted slivered almonds. Preparation time 45 minutes.

Yield: 4–6 servings

LAZY CHICKEN

- 6 pieces of chicken, breast, legs, or thighs (your choice)
- 1 medium onion
- 3–4 potatoes
- 6 carrots
- 1 cup white wine
- 1 cup chicken broth
- 6 minced garlic cloves
- 1 teaspoon salt
- ½ teaspoon pepper
- 1 teaspoon thyme
- 3 tablespoons butter

Preheat oven to 500 degrees. Quarter the onion. Cut the unpeeled potatoes into chunks. Pare and slice carrots. Put chicken pieces and vegetables in a 9x13 inch baking dish. Mix wine, broth and garlic and pour over the chicken and vegetables. Sprinkle with salt, pepper and thyme. Dot with butter. Reduce oven heat to 350 degrees and bake 1 hour. Turn chicken and vegetables as needed to brown. Add more chicken broth if necessary.

Yield: 6 servings

CHICKEN DELICIOUS

- 8 chicken breast halves
- 1½ cups chopped celery
- 1 8-ounce can drained sliced water chestnuts
- 1 10¾-ounce can cream of mushroom soup
- 1 cup mayonnaise
- 1 8-ounce package cornbread stuffing
- 1 teaspoon poultry seasoning
- ¾ cup melted margarine

Lightly grease a 3 quart baking dish. Cook chicken; skin, debone and cut into small bite size pieces. Mix soup, celery, mayonnaise and water chestnuts. Place chopped chicken in baking dish. Spoon soup mixture oven chicken. Mix stuffing, poultry seasoning and margarine; sprinkle over top. Bake 30 to 45 minutes at 350 degrees.

Yield: 10 servings

 *A mudskipper is really a fish with legs.*

BAKED CHICKEN SUPREME

- **2 frying size chickens or 8 halves large chicken breasts**
- **2 cups sour cream**
- **¼ cup lemon juice**
- **4 teaspoons Worcestershire sauce**
- **4 teaspoons celery salt**
- **2 teaspoons paprika**
- **4 minced cloves of garlic**
- **4 teaspoons salt**
- **½ teaspoon pepper**
- **1¾ cups packaged dry bread crumbs**
- **½ cup butter**
- **½ cup shortening**

Cut up whole chicken or use 8 halves of chicken breasts; wipe well with damp paper towel. Combine sour cream, lemon juice, Worcestershire, celery salt, paprika, garlic, salt and pepper and coat each piece well. Let stand covered in refrigerator overnight. Next day remove and roll in crumbs, coating evenly. Arrange in single layer in 9x13 inch baking dish. Melt butter and shortening and spoon over chicken. Bake uncovered at 350 degrees for 45 minutes to 1 hour. Remove to warm serving dish.

Yield: 8 servings

GOLDEN CHICKEN TRIANGLES

- **6 ounces softened cream cheese**
- **6 tablespoons melted margarine**
- **4 cups cooked, cubed chicken breasts**
- **½ teaspoon salt**
- **¼ teaspoon pepper**
- **4 tablespoons milk**
- **2 tablespoons chopped chives**
- **2 tablespoons chopped pimento**
- **2 8–ounce cans refrigerated quick crescent dinner rolls**
- **1½ cups seasoned crouton crumbs**

Heat oven to 350 degrees. In bowl, blend cheese and 4 tablespoons margarine until smooth. Add next 6 ingredients and mix well. Separate crescent dough into 8 rectangles. Firmly press perforations to seal. Spoon ½ cup meat mixture onto center of each rectangle. Put 4 corners to top of chicken mixture and twist slightly. Seal edges. Brush tops with 2 tablespoons melted margarine. Dip in crouton crumbs. Place on ungreased cookie sheet. Bake at 350 degrees for 20–25 minutes until golden brown.

Yield: 8 servings

LUNCHEON CHICKEN

- 6 chicken breast halves
- 1 medium chopped onion
- 3 tablespoons butter
- 1½ cups chicken broth
- 2 10¾–ounce cans cream of chicken soup
- 1 10¾–ounce can cream of mushroom soup
- 1 2–ounce jar diced pimentos
- 1 16–ounce can drained green peas
- 2 boxes of frozen Pepperidge Farm pastry cups
- ½ teaspoon salt to taste
- ¼ teaspoon pepper or to taste

Heat oven to 350 degrees. Place chicken breasts in a foil-lined baking dish. Cover with foil and bake for 40 minutes. When cool, skin, debone and slice into bite size pieces. Sauté chopped onion in butter. Add chicken broth, cream of chicken and mushroom soup and mix. Stir in the chicken pieces, pimentos, and green peas. Heat thoroughly. Salt and pepper to taste. Serve in cooked pastry cups.

Yield: 12 servings

CHICKEN SPAGHETTI

- 1 3 to 4 pound chicken
- 1 8–ounce package spaghetti
- ½ cup margarine
- 1 cup chopped celery
- 1 chopped onion
- 1 cup sliced fresh mushrooms or 1 4–ounce can
- ½ cup chopped green bell pepper
- 1 minced garlic clove
- ½ teaspoon cayenne pepper
- 1 teaspoon chili powder
- 2 cups of tomatoes
- ½ pound Velveeta cheese
- ½ teaspoon salt to taste
- ¼ teaspoon pepper to taste

Boil chicken, skin, debone and chop into bite size pieces. Reserve 1 cup broth if needed for final dish. Cook spaghetti according to box direction using remaining broth. Melt margarine and add celery, onion, green pepper, garlic, cayenne, chili powder, and mushrooms. Cook until tender. Purée tomatoes and cut cheese into small hunks. Add to above mixture with salt and pepper to taste. Continue to cook for about 20 minutes. Add spaghetti and turn into a 4 quart baking dish. Mixture should be soupy; if not, add reserved broth to the desired consistency. Bake in a 4 quart baking dish for approximately 30 minutes.

Yield: 12 servings

CHICKEN LASAGNA

9 uncooked lasagna noodles
¼ cup butter or margarine
8 ounces sliced fresh mushrooms
2 large cloves of garlic, minced
1 teaspoon lemon juice
¼ cup flour
½ teaspoon salt
2 teaspoons instant chicken bouillon
3 cups milk
3 cups diced cooked chicken
¾ cup chopped fresh parsley
¼ cup grated Parmesan cheese
1 15–ounce carton ricotta cheese
2 cups shredded mozzarella cheese
1 cup Parmesan cheese

Cook lasagna noodles al dente. Drain and rinse. In large saucepan melt margarine. Add mushrooms, garlic, salt and lemon juice. Sauté until tender, about 5 minutes. Stir in flour and blend well. Mix chicken bouillon with the milk and add to the mushroom mixture. Cook over medium heat until it thickens, stirring constantly. Stir in the chicken and ½ cup chopped parsley, reserving the remaining parsley to sprinkle over the top after it has baked.

To assemble: Spread ⅓ of chicken sauce in an ungreased 9x13 inch baking dish. Place 3 lasagna noodles over this. Spread with ⅓ of ricotta cheese. Sprinkle with ⅓ of mozzarella cheese and ⅓ of Parmesan cheese. Repeat layers. Cover with foil and place in a preheated 325 degree oven. Bake for 45 minutes. Remove from oven and sprinkle remaining parsley over the top. Let stand for 10 to 15 minutes before serving.

Yield: 8 servings

CHICKEN AND HAM ROLL UPS

6 boneless and skinless chicken breast halves
6 thin slices of ham
6 slices Swiss cheese
3 chicken bouillon cubes
2 cups hot water
2 tablespoons cornstarch
¼ cup margarine

Pound the skinned and boned chicken breasts to ¼ inch. Place ham and cheese slices in center of breast. Roll up and secure with tooth picks. Sauté breasts in skillet with margarine, turning often, until browned on all sides. Dissolve chicken bouillon in hot water and add to chicken in skillet. Cover and simmer 30 minutes. Dissolve cornstarch in ¼ cup water. Add to chicken mixture to thicken. Serve chicken on a platter and serve with gravy on the side.

Yield: 6 servings

GOTTA LOVE 'EM!
EASY CHICKEN CRESCENTS

- 1 5-ounce can drained chicken
- 1 8-ounce package cream cheese
- 3 tablespoons dried minced onion
- ½ cup chopped pecans or slivered almonds
- ⅓ cup mayonnaise
- 1 8-ounce can crescent rolls
- ½ cup melted margarine or butter
- ½ cup commercial fine bread crumbs

Combine first 5 ingredients, mix until creamy. Separate rolls. Divide chicken mixture into eighths. Mold into football shapes and center each lengthwise on a dough triangle. Stretch short ends of dough as necessary to accommodate chicken and fold corners to center so they overlap. Roll long end of dough up and over, diaper fashion. Manipulate dough and filling so seams are sealed and roll takes on a smooth egg shape. Roll in margarine, then in crumbs. Place rolls in a 9x11 baking dish that has been sprayed with vegetable oil. Bake at 350 degrees for 25 to 35 minutes or until bread is done and golden brown. Drizzle sauce over rolls and garnish with fresh parsley.

SAUCE:

- 1 10 ounce can cream of chicken soup
- ½ cup water

Combine soup and water and heat.

Yield: 4 servings

Note: Filling may be made ahead of time. Leftovers heat nicely in oven (not microwave).

PARTY CHICKEN

- 8 boneless and skinless chicken breast halves
- 8 slices of bacon
- 1 package chipped beef
- 1 10¾-ounce can undiluted mushroom soup
- ½ pint sour cream

Wrap each breast with a slice of bacon. Cover bottom of flat greased 8x12x2 inch baking dish with chipped beef. Place chicken breasts on top of beef. Mix soup and sour cream and pour over the chicken. Bake at 275 degrees for 3 hours uncovered. May be prepared ahead of time. Refrigerate until ready to cook.

Yield: 8 servings

TURKEY SATAYS WITH PEANUT SAUCE

2 pounds skinned turkey breast
1 cup plain low-fat yogurt
½ cup safflower oil
1 tablespoon grated fresh ginger
½ teaspoon ground cardamom
½ teaspoon ground coriander
¼ teaspoon salt
½ teaspoon freshly ground black pepper
2 teaspoons paprika

Whisk yogurt and remaining ingredients together for the marinade. Cut turkey into 1 inch cubes, and refrigerate for 6 hours or overnight, stirring occasionally to keep pieces well coated. If you plan to grill the turkey, light coals about 30 minutes before cooking. For broiling, preheat broiler with rack and pan in place about 10 minutes beforehand. Thread the turkey cubes onto skewer (preferably with square or flat blades), so the cubes will not slip when turned and cook unevenly. Grill cubes over hot coals turning several times for 8 minutes. Broiling may take as long as 15 minutes, or as little as 4 minutes each side. To test for doneness, make a small cut in turkey to see if it has turned from pink to white. Arrange the satays on a heated platter and serve with peanut sauce.

PEANUT SAUCE:
⅓ cup peanut butter
1 cup boiling water
2 finely chopped garlic cloves
2 tablespoons fresh lemon juice
2 tablespoon low-sodium soy sauce
¼ teaspoon crushed red pepper
1 tablespoon molasses

Heat peanut butter in heavy bottom saucepan over low heat. Whisk in boiling water, then stir in garlic, lemon juice, soy sauce, red pepper and molasses. Bring the mixture to boil and whisk it until it thickens, about 2 minutes. Taste and add more red pepper or molasses if desired. Pour in a sauceboat.

Yield: 8 servings

 *Buttercups can grow up to 3 feet high.*

TURKEY CUTLETS WITH BALSAMIC–BROWN SUGAR SAUCE

¼ cup all purpose flour
1 teaspoon salt
1 teaspoon dried thyme
½ teaspoon pepper
4 4–ounce turkey cutlets
1 tablespoon olive oil
¼ cup minced shallots
⅔ cup dry red wine
⅔ cup low–salt chicken broth
¼ cup balsamic vinegar
2 tablespoons brown sugar
¼ teaspoon salt
thyme sprigs (optional)

Combine the first 4 ingredients in a shallow dish; stir well. Dredge turkey cutlets in flour mixture. Heat oil in a large nonstick skillet over medium heat. Add cutlets, and cook 3 minutes on each side or until done. Remove cutlets to a serving platter; set aside, and keep warm. Add shallots to skillet, and sauté over medium heat for 1 minute. Add wine and broth; stir, scraping bottom of skillet with a wooden spoon to loosen the browned bits. Bring to a boil, and cook for 5 minutes. Add vinegar, sugar and ¼ teaspoon salt; bring to a boil. Reduce heat, and simmer for 3 minutes. Spoon sauce over cutlets. Garnish with thyme sprigs if desired.

Yield: 4 servings

TURKEY BREAST IN PIQUANT SAUCE

4–5 pound turkey breast
½ cup all purpose flour
8 tablespoons unsalted butter
1 tablespoon olive oil
½ cup dry white wine
juice of 1 lemon
salt and pepper to taste

Slice turkey breast into 12 thin slices about ⅛ inch thick. Pound gently with side of big butcher knife. Dust breasts with flour, patting it on to make sure it sticks. Melt butter in large skillet over medium heat. Add olive oil to prevent burning. Sauté slices about 3 minutes; turn and cook 3 more minutes. Depending on the size of skillets, it will be necessary to cook slices in 2 or 3 batches. Remove each batch, keeping warm until all are cooked. Add wine and lemon juice to the skillet pan, stirring to incorporate the remaining browned butter and juices. Add salt. Put all slices back in pan, coating each with sauce. Simmer for 2 minutes. Serve hot with sauce.

Yield: 8 servings

SMOKED TURKEY

1 cup margarine
4 tablespoons lemon juice
1 tablespoon Worcestershire sauce
2 tablespoons French salad dressing
1 tablespoon liquid smoke
1 teaspoon garlic salt
1 teaspoon lemon pepper
1 10–12 pound turkey

Wash turkey and pat dry with paper towels. Melt margarine in a small container; add remaining ingredients, mixing well. Place turkey in a 9x13 inch baking pan and brush with sauce. Cook for 4 to 6 hours at 300 degrees, basting often. This is excellent if cooked in a smoker or covered charcoal grill.

Yield: 8–10 servings

QUICK AND EASY CATFISH FILLET

1 pound catfish fillets
¼ cup cornmeal
¼ cup seasoned bread crumbs
½ teaspoon paprika
½ cup milk
2 tablespoon melted margarine

Combine cornmeal and seasoned bread crumbs with paprika. Dip catfish fillets in milk and coat with the cornmeal bread crumb mixture. Place fish on an oiled baking pan. Drizzle with melted margarine. Bake at 450 degrees for 12 to 15 minutes or until fish flakes.

Yield: 4 servings

BEER BATTER SHRIMP

24 jumbo shrimp
1½ cups all purpose flour
1½ cups beer
½ teaspoon salt (or to taste)

Butterfly shrimp. Leave tail on. Combine flour, beer, salt and blend until smooth. Dip shrimp in batter. Fry in vegetable oil until golden, 2 to 3 minutes each side. Drain on paper towels. Dip in sauce.

SAUCE:
1 cup orange marmalade
2 tablespoons horseradish
⅛ teaspoon grated ginger (or to taste)

Combine all ingredients.

Yield: 4 servings

SHRIMP FAJITAS

- **1 pound medium shelled shrimp**
- **2 tablespoons chopped cilantro**
- **1 teaspoon salt**
- **2 teaspoons seasoning salt**
- **¼ teaspoon Tabasco (optional)**
- **½ cup fresh or canned corn**
- **⅓ cup fresh chopped tomato**
- **3 green onions**
- **1 yellow or red bell pepper**
- **1 package flour or corn tortillas**

Spray a large deep skillet with cooking spray. Season shrimp. Cut green onions in 1 inch pieces, include green tops. Thinly slice bell pepper. Place shrimp and vegetables in skillet and sauté on medium to high heat, approximately 5 minutes or until shrimp turns pink, stirring constantly. Heat flour tortillas on a very hot grill for a few seconds until soft and warm. Roll shrimp mixture and serve immediately or serve shrimp mixture on a warm platter and let each make their own.

Yield: 4 servings

 *Every year spiny lobsters march across the ocean floor in single file to reach deeper water.*

SHRIMP AND WILD RICE

- **2 boxes wild rice and long grain rice**
- **1 tablespoon butter**
- **1 pound fresh sliced mushrooms**
- **2 cups diced celery**
- **2 cups onions**
- **½ cup green pepper**
- **¼ cup margarine**
- **1¼ pounds cooked shrimp**
- **½ cup almonds**
- **3 10¾-ounce cans mushroom soup**
- **½ teaspoon garlic powder (or to taste)**

Cook rice as directed on box. Add 1 tablespoon butter after cooking. Sauté mushrooms, celery, onions, green peppers in ¼ cup margarine, add garlic powder to taste. When vegetables are tender (do not let them brown), pour into a casserole sprayed with vegetable oil. Add cooked shrimp. Mix well, add soup and cooked rice and almonds. Bake covered for 45 minutes at 350 degrees. Uncover and bake an additional 15 minutes.

Yield: 12 servings

CREAMED SHRIMP

1 pound unpeeled medium size shrimp
¼ cup butter or margarine
½ cup chopped onion
½ cup chopped sweet red or green pepper
1 10–ounce can cream of mushroom soup
½ cup water
¼ teaspoon pepper
⅛ teaspoon red pepper
1 teaspoon Creole seasoning

Melt butter or margarine over medium heat; add onion and chopped peppers. Stir in undiluted soup and the next 4 ingredients. Bring mixture to a boil, stirring constantly. Add shrimp and simmer 10 minutes. Serve over rice.

Yield: 4 servings

SHRIMPLY SENSATIONAL

½ cup butter or margarine
6 garlic cloves
½ lemon, squeezed for juice
2 tablespoons Worcestershire sauce
2 pounds peeled medium large shrimp
¼ cup dried onion flakes
¼ teaspoon each: chili powder, paprika, seasoning salt, pepper, cayenne, celery salt, thyme, rosemary, dried parsley

Melt butter. Pour in a casserole or baking dish; add juice and any pulp from the lemon, Worcestershire and shrimp. Mix to coat shrimp. Season generously with spices. Cover with foil and bake 10 to 20 minutes at 375 degrees or until shrimp is pink. Add more butter or margarine for dipping if needed. Serve with French bread.

Yield: 8 servings

TEXAS TUNA MOLD

2 6–ounce cans drained white tuna
6 chopped hard boiled eggs
½ cup chopped stuffed olive
2 tablespoons gelatin
½ cup vermouth
2 cups mayonnaise (room temperature)

Flake tuna and add chopped eggs and olives. Dissolve gelatin in vermouth over hot water; stir in mayonnaise. Fold in tuna, chopped eggs and olives. Pour into oiled mold and chill at least 6 hours in refrigerator. Do not freeze.

Yield: 8 servings

TUNA NOODLE CASSEROLE

- **1 6–ounce package medium noodles**
- **1 6–ounce can drained tuna**
- **½ cup mayonnaise**
- **1 cup sliced celery**
- **⅓ cup chopped onion**
- **½ cup diced green pepper**
- **¼ cup chopped pimento**
- **1 teaspoon salt**
- **1 10¾–ounce cream of celery soup**
- **½ cup milk**
- **1 cup shredded Cheddar cheese**
- **½ cup slivered blanched almonds**

Cook noodles in boiling salted water and drain. Combine noodles, tuna, mayonnaise, vegetables and salt. Blend soup and milk; heat thoroughly. Add cheese and stir until it melts. Remove from heat and add noodles; mix well. Turn into 1½ quart casserole dish and top with almonds. Bake for 20 minutes at 400 degrees or until bubbly.

Yield: 8–10 servings

SALMON PATTIES

- **1 14¾–ounce can drained pink salmon**
- **½ cup evaporated milk**
- **1½ cups bread crumbs**
- **¼ cup dill pickle relish**
- **¼ cup finely chopped celery**
- **3 tablespoons finely chopped onion**

Debone and flake the drained pink salmon and place in a medium bowl. Add ½ cup milk, ½ cup crumbs, relish, celery and onion; mix well. With wet hands, shape ¼ cupfuls into patties. Dip in remaining milk, then remaining crumbs. Heat oil and fry a few at a time for 2 to 2½ minutes or until golden brown. Drain on paper towel. Serve with Tartar Sauce

TARTAR SAUCE:

- **⅔ cup evaporated milk**
- **¼ cup mayonnaise**
- **2 tablespoons dill pickle relish**
- **1 tablespoon finely chopped onion**

Combine ingredients in a medium saucepan; cook over medium–low heat until heated through and slightly thickened. Serve warm with patties.

Yield: 4–6 servings

GRILLED SALMON

2 1 pound salmon fillets
½ cup vegetable oil
½ cup lemon juice
4 thinly sliced green onions
3 tablespoons minced fresh parsley
1 teaspoon minced fresh rosemary or ½ teaspoon dried rosemary
½ teaspoon salt
⅛ teaspoon pepper

Place salmon in a shallow dish. Combine remaining ingredients and mix well. Set aside ¼ cup for basting; pour the rest over the salmon. Cover and refrigerate for 30 minutes. Drain, discarding marinade. Grill salmon over medium coals skin side down, for 15 to 20 minutes or until fish flakes easily with a fork. Baste occasionally with reserved marinade.

Yield: 4 servings

SOLE IN HERBED BUTTER

4 tablespoons butter or margarine, softened
1 teaspoon dill weed
½ teaspoon onion powder
½ teaspoon garlic powder
½ teaspoon salt, optional
¼ teaspoon white pepper
2 pounds sole fillets
fresh dill and lemon wedges (optional)

In a bowl, mix butter, dill, onion powder, garlic powder, salt and pepper. Transfer to a skillet; heat on medium heat until melted. Add sole and sauté for several minutes on each side or until it flakes easily with a fork. Garnish with dill and lemon.

Yield: 6 servings

BAKED LEMON HADDOCK

2 pounds haddock fillets
1 cup seasoned dry bread crumbs
¼ cup melted butter or margarine
2 tablespoons dried parsley flakes
2 teaspoons grated lemon peel
½ teaspoon garlic powder

Cut fish into serving–size pieces. Place in a greased 8x12 inch baking dish. Combine remaining ingredients; sprinkle over fish. Bake at 350 degrees for 25 minutes or until fish flakes easily with a fork.

Yield: 6 servings

CRAB CASSEROLE

- **8 slices bread**
- **2 cups crab meat**
- **½ cup mayonnaise**
- **1 chopped onion**
- **1 chopped green pepper**
- **1 cup chopped celery**
- **4 beaten eggs**
- **3 cups milk**
- **1 10¾-ounce can mushroom soup**
- **1½ cups grated cheese**
- **paprika**

Dice half the bread, place in 9x13 inch baking dish. Mix crab, mayonnaise, onion, green pepper, and celery; spread over bread. Trim crust from remaining bread; cut in half. Place over crab mixture. Mix eggs and milk; pour in baking dish. Let stand overnight in refrigerator. Bake at 325 degrees for 15 minutes. Remove from oven; spoon soup over top. Add cheese and sprinkle with paprika. Bake 1 hour longer.

Yield: 12 servings

Note: Two chicken breasts can be substituted for crab.

SWEET AND SOUR PORK

- **1 pound pork tenderloin**
- **2 8-ounce cans pineapple tidbits**
- **⅓ cup ketchup**
- **2 tablespoons each soy sauce, vinegar, brown sugar**
- **¾ teaspoon salt**
- **¼ teaspoon pepper**
- **¼ teaspoon ground ginger**
- **⅓ cup water**
- **2 tablespoons cornstarch**
- **2 tablespoons cooking oil**
- **1 medium chopped onion**
- **1 thinly sliced green pepper**
- **hot cooked rice**

Cut the tenderloin into 1½ x ¼ inch strips; set aside. Drain pineapple, reserving juice in a small bowl. Set pineapple aside. Mix cornstarch with water and stir into juice until smooth. Add ketchup, soy sauce, vinegar, brown sugar, salt, pepper and ginger to this and blend. Heat oil in a large skillet or wok on high; stir-fry pork and onion for 5 to 7 minutes or until pork is no longer pink. Stir pineapple juice mixture; add to the skillet. Cook and stir until thickened and bubbly. Add pineapple and green pepper. Reduce heat; cover and cook for 5 minutes more. Serve immediately over rice.

Yield: 4 servings

EASY CRANBERRY PORK CHOPS

6 pork chops
1 16-ounce can whole cranberry sauce
1 10¾-ounce can cream of mushroom soup

Brown pork chops in small amount of shortening in Dutch oven. Pour cranberry sauce over chops and cover with soup. Bake covered for 45 minutes at 350 degrees or until chops are tender.

Yield: 6 servings

LAURIE'S CHINESE PORK

2 12-ounce pork tenderloins
1 green onion
1 clove crushed garlic
¼ cup light soy sauce
2 tablespoons dry red wine
1 tablespoon brown sugar
1 tablespoon honey
½ teaspoon cinnamon

Cut green onion in half and mix with, garlic, soy sauce, wine, brown sugar, honey, cinnamon to marinate pork tenderloins. Bake for 45 minutes at 350 degrees basting frequently.

Yield: 6 servings

Note: Good cooked on a grill.

HAM ALMOND CASSEROLE

1½ cups uncooked noodles
½ cup milk
1 10¾-ounce can Cheddar cheese soup
1 tablespoon grated onion
½ cup chopped celery
½ cup finely chopped green pepper
1 3-ounce can mushrooms
½ cup salted almonds
2 cups diced ham
¼ cup sliced ripe olives
½ cup buttered bread crumbs
¼ teaspoon pepper

Cook noodles as directed on package. Add milk to soup to make a smooth sauce. Add onion, celery, green pepper, mushrooms, almonds and olives to the sauce. Stir in the noodles, ham and desired seasonings. Pour into greased 2 quart casserole; top with crumbs. Bake for 30 minutes at 375 degrees.

Yield: 8 servings

SAUSAGE CASSEROLE

1 pound bulk sausage
1 cup chopped celery
½ cup chopped onion
½ cup chopped green pepper
2 tablespoons sausage drippings
1 5-ounce can drained sliced water chestnuts
1 4-ounce can drained mushrooms pieces and stems
3 cups cooked rice
1½ packages dehydrated chicken noodle soup
2½ cups water
⅓ cup slivered toasted almonds (optional)

Lightly brown sausage in a skillet. Remove and drain. Save 2 tablespoons of the drippings in the skillet and lightly sauté the celery , onion, and peppers. Return the sausage to the skillet and add water chestnuts, mushrooms, rice, chicken noodle soup and water. Mix and put in a 3 quart baking dish; top with slivered almonds. Cover and bake for 1 hour at 350 degrees. Remove cover and bake another 15 minutes.

Yield: 8 servings

HAM VEGGIE MEDLEY

3 cups cubed ham
1 pound thinly sliced yellow squash (fresh or frozen)
1 pound thinly sliced zucchini squash
½ cup chopped onion
1 cup shredded carrots
1 10¾-ounce can cream of celery soup
1 cup sour cream
1 teaspoon Greek seasoning
1 8-ounce package herb stuffing mix
½ cup melted margarine

Steam or simmer fresh squash until tender. If using frozen squash, thaw and drain. Mix squash, ham, onion, carrots, soup, sour cream and seasoning together. Combine melted margarine with stuffing. Spread ½ stuffing in bottom of a 9x13 inch baking dish. Spoon ham-veggie mixture on top of stuffing. Put remaining stuffing over top of veggie layer. Bake 30 to 40 minutes or until golden brown at 350 degrees.

Yield: 8–10 servings

HAM ROLLUPS WITH CHEESE SPREAD AND CUMBERLAND SAUCE

- **1 8–ounce package cream cheese**
- **¼ cup mayonnaise**
- **⅛ cup finely chopped green pepper**
- **¼ cup chopped pimento**
- **2 tablespoons finely chopped onion**
- **1 pound thinly sliced ham (approximately ⅛ inch thick)**

Combine softened cream cheese and mayonnaise; mix until blended. Add green pepper, pimento and onion; mix well. Makes 1¾ cups. Spread cheese on ham slices and roll up securing with a toothpick. Top with Cranberry Cumberland Sauce (page 80).

Yield: 20 servings

Note: Approximately 20 (⅛ inch) slices per pound.

PEPPERCORN CRUSTED PORK LOIN ROAST

- **1 2½ pound lean pork loin boneless roast**
- **3 tablespoons Dijon mustard**
- **1 tablespoon non fat buttermilk**
- **2 cups soft whole wheat bread crumbs**
- **2 tablespoons cracked pepper**
- **2 teaspoons crushed assorted peppercorns**
- **2 teaspoons chopped fresh thyme**
- **¼ teaspoon salt**

Combine mustard and buttermilk; spread over roast. Combine bread crumbs with cracked pepper, crushed assorted peppercorns, thyme and salt; press evenly onto roast. Place on a rack in a roasting pan coated with cooking spray. Insert meat thermometer into thickest part. Bake for 2 hours at 325 degrees or until thermometer registers 160 degrees. Let stand 10 minutes before slicing. Serve with Creamy Peppercorn Sauce

CREAMY PEPPERCORN SAUCE:

- **¾ cup non fat buttermilk**
- **⅓ cup light sour cream (or non fat)**
- **3 tablespoons grated Parmesan cheese**
- **3 tablespoons reduced fat mayonnaise**
- **1½ tablespoons lemon juice**
- **1½ teaspoons whole assorted crushed peppercorns**
- **¼ teaspoon salt**

Mix together and serve over roast.

Yield: 8 servings

OAHU PORK

2½ pounds cubed pork butt
2 teaspoons soy sauce
½ teaspoon salt
2 tablespoons cornstarch
2 tablespoons whiskey
1 teaspoon sugar
2 cloves minced garlic
⅓ cup ketchup
⅔ cup water
2 tablespoons cornstarch
1 tablespoon vinegar
2 tablespoons brown sugar
2 tablespoons canola oil
sesame seeds

Mix soy sauce, salt, cornstarch, whiskey, sugar and minced garlic. Pour over the cubed pork and set aside for 15 to 30 minutes. Mix water and remaining 2 tablespoons cornstarch together; add ketchup, vinegar and brown sugar and put in large pot and simmer. Brown the cubed pork in a skillet with 2 tablespoons canola oil. When browned, add it to the ketchup, vinegar and brown sugar mixture and simmer for 45–60 minutes. Sprinkle with sesame seeds and serve over cooked rice.

Yield: 8 servings

ROAST PORK WITH SAUERKRAUT

1 pork roast, any size
2 tablespoons oil
2 15–ounce cans undrained Bavarian style sauerkraut
½ cup dried apricots
1 quartered onion
1 sliced and seeded apple
pepper to taste

Heat oil in a Dutch oven, and brown pork roast on all sides. Add the sauerkraut, apricots, onion, apple and pepper. Bake at 350 degrees for 3 to 4 hours until meat is very tender.

Yield: 6 servings

SPICED PORK TENDERLOIN

¾ cup olive oil
3 tablespoons minced garlic
4½ teaspoons ground cumin
1½ teaspoons cayenne pepper
1½ teaspoons ground cinnamon
3 pounds pork tenderloin
2 tablespoons olive oil

Combine ¾ cup olive oil, garlic, cumin, cayenne pepper, and cinnamon in a bowl. Rub over pork. Cover pork and refrigerate at least 4 hours or overnight. In the 2 tablespoons of olive oil, brown pork on all sides. Remove and bake in preheated 400 degree oven for 15 or 20 minutes. Slice and serve.

Yield: 4 servings

CRANBERRY GLAZED PORK LOIN

1 3 pound boneless pork loin
1 large chopped onion
5 sliced carrots
⅓ cup cranberry juice
2 tablespoons Bouquet Garni
salt and pepper to taste

Put vegetables in bottom of a roasting pan. Rinse the pork loin in cool water and pat dry. Roll loin in the Bouquet Garni and place on top of the vegetables. Roast for 15 minutes at 425 degrees. Reduce heat to 350 degrees. Add the cranberry juice and cook for 60 to 70 minutes until done. Baste often. Serve on top of vegetables.

Yield: 6 servings

PORK TENDERLOIN IN HOISIN SAUCE

1 2½ pound pork tenderloin
1 teaspoon chopped garlic
2 tablespoons sesame oil
2 tablespoons soy sauce
1 tablespoon sherry
3 tablespoons hoisin sauce
2 tablespoons honey or corn syrup (divided use)

Combine garlic, oil, soy, sherry, hoisin, and 1 tablespoon honey and pour over pork loin. Marinate 3 hours. Place on an oiled broiler pan with water in the bottom section. Bake 450 degrees for 20 minutes. Reduce heat to 350 degrees and bake 30 minutes, basting with the remaining sauce to which the remaining tablespoon of honey has been added.

Yield: 5 servings

 *An armadillo can walk across the bottom of a river to cross to the other side.*

VEAL SCALLOPPINE

- **1 pound thinly sliced veal**
- **2 tablespoons olive oil**
- **2–3 tablespoons butter (divided)**
- **1 pound thinly sliced fresh mushrooms**
- **½ cup white wine**
- **¼ cup chicken broth**

Lightly flour veal. In a skillet quickly brown veal (scalloppine) in hot oil and ½ butter. Place in small 8x8 inch baking dish; salt and pepper to taste. Add remaining butter to skillet and sauté mushrooms until golden (5 minutes). Pour over veal. Mix wine and broth with crumblies in the skillet and let simmer about 2 minutes. Pour over veal. Cover and cook 30 minutes at 325 degrees. Serve over noodles or rice. No substitute for thin scalloppine.

Yield: 4 servings

Note: Have butcher slice veal no more than ¼ inch thick.

VEAL SHANKS

- **8 veal shanks**
- **¼ cup olive oil or vegetable oil**
- **¼ teaspoon salt**
- **¼ teaspoon pepper**
- **⅛ teaspoon garlic powder**
- **1 cup flour**
- **2 medium diced onions**
- **4 cloves diced garlic**
- **3–4 ribs of celery, chopped**
- **½ medium diced bell pepper**
- **5–6 medium mushrooms (optional)**
- **1 14½–ounce can chicken broth**
- **1 8–ounce can tomato sauce**
- **rosemary and thyme to taste**
- **1 small package baby carrots**

Dredge shanks in seasoned flour and sauté in oil. Remove when brown. Sauté vegetables in oil. Add tomato sauce and chicken broth and rosemary and thyme to taste. Cook shanks and vegetables together until shanks are fork tender.

Yield: 8 servings

Note: If desired can add ¼ cup red or white wine while cooking.

VEAL PARMIGIANA

- **1 cup packaged bread crumbs**
- **¼ cup grated Parmesan cheese**
- **12 thin slices veal**
- **2 eggs, slightly beaten**
- **1 cup chopped onion**
- **1 clove mashed garlic**
- **2 tablespoons olive or vegetable oil**
- **1 16–ounce can tomatoes**
- **2 8–ounce cans tomato sauce**
- **1½ teaspoons crumbled basil leaf**
- **½ teaspoon crumbled thyme leaf**
- **½ teaspoon salt**
- **½ teaspoon onion salt**
- **¼ teaspoon pepper**
- **2 tablespoons olive or vegetable oil**
- **2 tablespoons butter or margarine**
- **1 8–ounce package mozzarella cheese**
- **½ cup grated Parmesan cheese**

Mix bread crumbs and ¼ cup Parmesan cheese. Dip veal slices in beaten egg; coat well with crumb mixture. Let stand to dry (this helps keep coating on veal) while preparing sauce. Sauté onion and garlic in 2 tablespoon oil in saucepan until soft. Add tomatoes, tomato sauce, basil, thyme, salts, pepper. Cover; simmer 15 minutes. Heat oven to 350 degrees. Heat 2 tablespoon oil and butter in skillet until mixture foams. Add veal slices a few at a time; brown on both sides. Remove from skillet and place in a shallow 8x12 inch baking dish. Slice mozzarella cheese. Layer cheese and pour sauce over top. Sprinkle with ½ cup Parmesan cheese. Bake 15 to 20 minutes or until sauce bubbles and cheese melts.

Yield: 6 servings

 *There are 20 different species of armadillo.*

Eggs, Cheese & Pasta

FARMER'S BREAKFAST

- 3 cups frozen hash brown potatoes with onions and peppers
- ¾ cup shredded Monterey Jack cheese with jalapeños
- 1 cup diced cooked ham
- 4 beaten eggs
- 1 12-ounce can evaporated skim milk
- salt and pepper to taste

Grease 2 quart baking dish; arrange potatoes on bottom. Sprinkle with cheese and ham. Combine eggs, milk, salt and pepper and pour over potato mixture. Cover and refrigerate overnight. Bake uncovered at 350 degrees for 40–45 minutes.

Yield: 6 servings

SUNDAY BRUNCH CASSEROLE

- 2¼ cups seasoned croutons
- 1½ pounds seasoned sausage
- 4 eggs
- 2¼ cups milk
- 1 10-ounce can cream of mushroom soup
- 1 4-ounce can drained chopped mushrooms
- ½ teaspoon dry mustard
- 2 cups grated Cheddar cheese

Lightly grease a 9x13 inch baking dish. Cook sausage and drain well. Spread croutons evenly over bottom of dish; spread cooked sausage over croutons. Beat eggs with milk and add remaining ingredients, except cheese. Pour over sausage and croutons. Cover and refrigerate overnight. Bake uncovered at 325 degrees 55–60 minutes. Sprinkle with cheese and bake additional 5 minutes.

Yield: 10–12 servings

Note: Especially good served with picante sauce.

EGG AND SAUSAGE SOUFFLÉ

- 6 slightly beaten eggs
- 6 slices cubed bread
- 1 cup shredded Cheddar cheese
- 1 pound pork sausage
- 2 cups milk
- 1 teaspoon salt
- 1 teaspoon dry mustard
- 1 pound sautéed and cooled mushrooms

Cook sausage and drain. Beat eggs and mix together all ingredients. Pour into a 1½ quart baking dish; refrigerate overnight. Bake uncovered at 350 degrees 50–60 minutes.

Yield: 12 servings

FANCY BRUNCH EGGS

6–9 hard boiled eggs
2 teaspoons prepared mustard
3 tablespoons sour cream
1 teaspoon vinegar
¼ teaspoon salt
⅛ teaspoon white pepper

Cut eggs in half lengthwise; remove yolks. Mash yolks with other ingredients; adjust seasonings to taste. Fill egg whites with yolk mixture and arrange in casserole dish, yolk side up.

SAUCE:
⅓ cup finely chopped onion
½ cup finely chopped green pepper
2 tablespoons margarine
¼ cup chopped pimento
1 10¾-ounce can cream of mushroom soup
¾ cup sour cream
½ cup grated sharp Cheddar cheese

Sauté onions and green peppers in margarine. Add pimento, soup and sour cream. Pour sauce over eggs; top with cheese. Bake at 350 degrees 20 minutes or until bubbly.

Yield: 10–12 servings

RANDY'S FAVORITE QUICHE

1 10 inch pie crust
4 slices crisply cooked bacon
4 chopped green onions
¼ pound thinly sliced ham
4 ounces shredded Swiss cheese
¼ pound thinly sliced turkey
4 ounces shredded Cheddar cheese
3 eggs
1 cup half and half

Bake pie crust at 450 degrees for 10 minutes; remove from oven. Crumble bacon over bottom of pie crust; add ham and Swiss cheese; add turkey and Cheddar cheese. Beat eggs and half and half together and pour over all ingredients. Let stand 10 minutes before baking. Bake at 350 degrees 30 minutes or until knife inserted in center comes out clean. Let stand 5 minutes before cutting.

Yield: 6 servings

ASPARAGUS HAM QUICHE

- **2 10-ounce packages frozen cut asparagus**
- **16 ounces chopped cooked ham**
- **2 cups shredded Swiss cheese**
- **½ cup finely chopped onion**
- **6 eggs**
- **2 cups milk**
- **1½ cups buttermilk baking mix**
- **2 tablespoons dried vegetable flakes**
- **¼ teaspoon pepper**

Thaw asparagus. Grease two 9 inch pie plates. Layer asparagus, ham, cheese and onion in pie plates. Beat eggs; add remaining ingredients and mix well. Divide mixture; pour half into each pie plate over asparagus. Bake at 375 degrees 45 minutes or until knife inserted in middle comes out clean.

Yield: 12 servings

SPINACH PIE SUPREME

- **3 10-ounce packages frozen chopped spinach**
- **2 6-ounce packages Muenster cheese slices**
- **1 small finely chopped onion**
- **1 cup reduced fat cottage cheese**
- **3 lightly beaten large eggs**
- **⅓ cup grated Parmesan cheese**
- **½ teaspoon salt**
- **¼ teaspoon pepper**

Thaw spinach and squeeze dry. Lightly grease pie plate and line with Muenster cheese slices. Combine spinach and remaining ingredients; mix well. Carefully pour into cheese lined pie plate. Bake at 350 degrees 45 minutes or until set. Cool 5–10 minutes before cutting.

Yield: 8 servings

Note: Bake on baking sheet or aluminum foil to catch any oil that might run over during baking.

 *Some species of lizard can grow new tails.*

GARDEN VEGETABLE PIE

2 cups finely chopped fresh broccoli
½ cup finely chopped onion
½ cup finely chopped green pepper
1 cup shredded Cheddar cheese
1½ cups milk
¾ cup baking mix
3 eggs
1 teaspoon salt
¼ teaspoon pepper

Grease a deep dish 10 inch pie plate. Mix broccoli, onion, green pepper and cheese; pour into pie plate. Beat remaining ingredients until smooth; pour over ingredients in pie plate. Preheat oven to 400 degrees and bake 35–40 minutes or until knife inserted in center comes out clean. Let stand 5 minutes before cutting.

Yield: 6–8 servings

Note: May substitute cauliflower for broccoli. If using fresh vegetables, cook in salted water for 5 minutes and drain thoroughly. If using frozen vegetables, thaw and drain.

PASTA WITH ONION SAUCE

3 ounces linguine or fettuccine
1½ cups fresh broccoli flowerets
non stick cooking spray
1 medium onion
¾ cup skim milk
2 teaspoons cornstarch
1 teaspoon instant chicken bouillon granules
dash pepper
dash nutmeg
2 tablespoons dry white wine
2 ounces shredded part skim mozzarella cheese

Cook pasta according to package directions; add broccoli last 5 minutes. Drain well. Spray large skillet with non stick spray. Slice onion and break into rings; add to skillet; cook 10 minutes over low heat or until tender. Mix together remaining ingredients except wine and cheese; add to onion in skillet. Cook and stir over medium heat until thick and bubbly. Cook and stir for 2 minutes longer; add wine and cheese; stir until cheese is melted. Pour cheese mixture over pasta and broccoli; toss and serve.

Yield: 5 servings

VEGETABLE LASAGNA

1 tablespoon vegetable oil
1 small chopped onion
3 minced garlic cloves
1 finely chopped carrot
1 finely chopped celery rib
2 cups sliced mushrooms
1 16–ounce can diced tomatoes
1 16–ounce can tomato sauce
2 tablespoons dried basil
2 tablespoons dried oregano
salt and freshly ground pepper, to taste
3 cups broccoli flowerets
9 lasagna noodles
1 cup low fat cottage cheese
3 cups low fat shredded mozzarella cheese
⅓ cup grated Parmesan cheese

In large saucepan, heat oil over medium heat; add onion and cook until tender; stir in garlic, carrot, celery and mushrooms; stir and cook 5 minutes. Add tomatoes; stir in tomato sauce, basil, oregano, salt and pepper to taste. Simmer 10 minutes or until slightly thickened. Cool; stir in broccoli.

Cook noodles according to package directions; rinse with cold water; drain. In lightly greased 9x13 inch baking dish, arrange 3 noodles evenly over bottom. Layer with one– half vegetable mixture; one–half cottage cheese; one–third mozzarella cheese. Starting with noodles, repeat layers ending with layer of noodles. Top with mozzarella and Parmesan cheese. Bake 350 degrees 35–45 minutes or until bubbly.

Yield: 8 Servings

 *The grasshopper can jump 20 times the length of its body.*

EMMA'S NOODLES

2 eggs
2 tablespoons milk
⅛ teaspoon salt
⅛ teaspoon pepper
1 cup flour
1 49½–ounce can chicken broth

Beat eggs, milk, salt and pepper until mixed. Add flour until mixture leaves sides of bowl; use extra flour, if needed. Roll mixture on floured surface and let sit 2 hours. Cut dough into strips. Heat chicken broth to boiling; add strips to broth, one at a time. Reduce heat and simmer 20 minutes.

Yield: 4 servings

CHICKEN PECAN FETTUCCINE

- ¼ cup butter
- 1 pound chicken breast
- 3 cups sliced fresh mushrooms
- 1 cup sliced green onions with tops
- ½ teaspoon salt
- ¼ teaspoon pepper
- ¼ teaspoon garlic powder
- 10 ounces fettuccine noodles
- ½ cup grated Parmesan cheese
- 1 cup chopped toasted pecans

SAUCE:

- ½ cup butter
- 1 egg yolk
- ⅔ cup half and half
- 2 tablespoons chopped fresh parsley
- ¼ teaspoon salt
- ¼ teaspoon pepper
- ¼ teaspoon garlic powder

Cut chicken breasts into ¾ inch chunks. Melt ¼ cup butter in large skillet; add chicken; sauté until lightly browned. Remove chicken from skillet; set aside. To pan drippings, add mushrooms, onion, salt, pepper and garlic powder; sauté until vegetables are tender. Add chicken; simmer 20 minutes or until chicken is tender. Cook fettuccine according to package directions; drain. Mix together sauce ingredients; add to fettuccine and stir well. Add chicken, vegetable mixture and Parmesan cheese. Garnish with toasted pecans; serve immediately.

Yield: 6 servings

PARMESAN SPINACH PASTA

- 8 ounces corkscrew macaroni
- 1 10–ounce package fresh spinach
- 1 cup salad oil
- ½ cup grated Parmesan cheese
- ¼ cup white vinegar
- ½ teaspoon salt
- ½ teaspoon pepper
- ¼ teaspoon ground cloves
- 1-2 minced garlic cloves
- 8 ounces cubed Mozzarella cheese

Cook macaroni according to package directions and drain; tear spinach. Place oil. cheese, vinegar, salt, pepper, cloves and garlic into blender and process until smooth. Chill. Just before serving, toss dressing with macaroni and spinach. Sprinkle with extra Parmesan cheese.

Yield: 8 servings

SPICY SHRIMP WITH GREEN FETTUCCINE

6 ounces green fettuccine noodles
1 tablespoon butter
2 cups sliced mushrooms
2 tablespoons sliced green onion
½ cup bottled clam juice
14 ounces peeled medium shrimp
1 cup low fat sour cream

SEASONING MIX:
¼ teaspoon salt
¼ teaspoon paprika
⅛ teaspoon onion powder
⅛ teaspoon red pepper
⅛ teaspoon black pepper
⅛ teaspoon white pepper
⅛ teaspoon thyme
⅛ teaspoon oregano

Cook noodles according to package directions; drain and keep warm. Blend seasoning mix; set aside. In large skillet, heat butter; add mushrooms and onions; cook 4 to 5 minutes. Add clam juice and bring to a boil; add shrimp; cook 3 to 4 minutes or until pink. Remove from heat and stir in sour cream and seasoning mix. Toss with noodles; sprinkle with Parmesan cheese; serve immediately.

Yield: 4 servings

CREAMY CRAWFISH FETTUCCINE

1 chopped green bell pepper
2 chopped medium onions
2 minced garlic cloves
¾ cup butter
¼ cup flour
1 pint half and half (divided use)
1 6–ounce roll garlic cheese
8 drops Tabasco sauce
½ teaspoon cayenne pepper
16 ounces thawed frozen crawfish tails (reserve liquid)
12 ounces fettuccine noodles
chopped parsley

Sauté bell pepper, onions and garlic in butter until onion is light brown. Gradually blend in flour, stirring constantly. Add ½ pint half and half; garlic cheese, broken into small pieces; continue stirring until cheese melts. Blend in remaining cream, Tabasco, pepper, crawfish and liquid. Mix well. Cook fettuccine according to package directions; drain. Pour creamy crawfish over noodles; garnish with parsley.

Yield: 6–8 servings

Note: May substitute fresh crawfish tails or shrimp; add ¼ cup shellfish stock.

Vegetables

ASPARAGUS MUSHROOM CASSEROLE

- **2 8–ounce packages frozen cut asparagus**
- **4 cups sliced fresh mushrooms**
- **1 cup chopped onions**
- **4 tablespoons butter or margarine**
- **2 tablespoons flour**
- **1 teaspoon chicken bouillon granules**
- **½ teaspoon salt and dash pepper**
- **½ teaspoon ground nutmeg**
- **1 cup milk**
- **¼ cup chopped pimento**
- **1½ teaspoons lemon juice**
- **¾ cup soft bread crumbs**
- **1 tablespoon melted butter or margarine**

Cook and drain asparagus; set aside. Cover and cook mushrooms and onions in butter about 10 minutes or until tender. Remove vegetables and leave butter in pan. Blend flour, bouillon, salt, pepper and nutmeg into butter. Add milk all at once; cook and stir until bubbly. Stir in mushrooms, onions, asparagus, pimento and lemon juice. Pour into 1½ quart baking dish. Combine bread crumbs and melted butter. Sprinkle over top. Bake at 350 degrees for 35–45 minutes.

Yield: 8–10 servings

ASPARAGUS GREEN PEA CASSEROLE

- **2 14½–ounce cans drained cut asparagus**
- **1 15–ounce can drained small green peas**
- **1 10¾–ounce can cream of mushroom soup**
- **1 cup grated Cheddar cheese (divided use)**
- **salt, pepper and butter to taste**
- **8–10 saltine crackers**

Mix asparagus, green peas, cream of mushroom soup, ¾ cup grated cheese, salt and pepper. Pour into 1½ quart baking dish. Crumble crackers over top. Dot with butter and sprinkle ¼ cup grated cheese over crackers. Bake at 350 degrees for 30–40 minutes or until bubbly and brown on top.

Yield: 6 servings

SUGARED ASPARAGUS

- **3 tablespoons butter or margarine**
- **3 tablespoons brown sugar**
- **2 pounds fresh asparagus**
- **1 cup chicken broth**

In a skillet over medium heat, stir butter and brown sugar until sugar is dissolved. Cut asparagus into 2 inch pieces and add to skillet; sauté for 2 minutes. Stir in chicken broth; bring to a boil. Reduce heat; cover and simmer 8–10 minutes or until asparagus is crisp–tender. Remove asparagus to a serving dish and keep warm. Cook sauce, uncovered, until reduced by half. Pour over asparagus and serve immediately.

Yield: 4–6 servings

SESAME BROCCOLI

- **1 pound fresh broccoli**
- **1 tablespoon salad oil**
- **1 tablespoon vinegar**
- **1 tablespoon soy sauce**
- **4 teaspoons sugar**
- **1 tablespoon toasted sesame seeds**

Cook broccoli until just tender. Heat last five ingredients and pour over hot broccoli.

Yield: 4–6 servings

BROCCOLI CASSEROLE

- **1 medium chopped onion**
- **2 tablespoons melted margarine**
- **1 10¾–ounce can cream of mushroom soup**
- **1 cup grated Cheddar cheese**
- **1 cup mayonnaise**
- **1 32–ounce package thawed frozen broccoli**
- **1 cup crumbled cheese crackers**

In a saucepan, sauté onion in margarine. Add mushroom soup, grated cheese and mayonnaise; warm to spreading consistency. Place broccoli in 2 quart baking dish and spread soup mixture over broccoli. Sprinkle crumbled cheese crackers over top. Bake uncovered at 375 degrees for 20–25 minutes or until bubbly.

Yield: 6–8 servings

CORN–BROCCOLI BAKE

- **1 10–ounce package frozen chopped broccoli**
- **½ cup melted butter**
- **1½ cups crushed Chicken in the Biskit crackers**
- **1 16–ounce can creamed corn**
- **1 7–ounce can drained whole kernel corn**
- **½ teaspoon salt**
- **¼ teaspoon pepper**

Thaw and drain broccoli. Mix butter and crackers and reserve ½ cup for topping. Mix ingredients and pour into 1½ quart baking dish; add topping. Bake at 350 degrees for 30 minutes.

Yield: 4–6 servings

CROCKPOT BEANS

- **½ pound fried and diced bacon**
- **2 tablespoons bacon drippings**
- **½ cup light brown sugar**
- **¼ cup cornstarch**
- **1 teaspoon dry mustard**
- **½ cup molasses**
- **1 tablespoon vinegar**
- **4 16–ounce cans baked beans**
- **1 chopped medium onion**
- **1 chopped green pepper**

Combine ingredients in a crockpot. Cover and cook on low for 8 hours.

Yield: 18 servings

CABBAGE SUPREME

- **1 beef bouillon cube**
- **¼ cup hot water**
- **5 cups shredded cabbage**
- **1 cup shredded carrots**
- **½ cup chopped green onion**
- **½ teaspoon salt**
- **½ teaspoon pepper**
- **¼ cup butter or margarine**
- **1 teaspoon prepared mustard**
- **½ cup chopped pecans**
- **¼ teaspoon paprika**

Dissolve bouillon in water and combine with cabbage, carrots, onion, salt and pepper in heavy saucepan; toss lightly. Cover and cook over low heat 5 minutes, stirring occasionally. Drain and set aside. Melt butter, stir in mustard and pecans and continue cooking for 2 minutes. Stir constantly. Pour over cabbage and sprinkle top with paprika.

Yield: 6 servings

EASY CORN PUDDING

- **1 17–ounce can cream style corn**
- **1 tablespoon sugar**
- **2 beaten eggs**
- **2 tablespoons melted margarine**
- **1 teaspoon salt**
- **⅛ teaspoon pepper**
- **1 teaspoon flour**
- **1 cup milk**

Add salt, sugar, pepper, flour and margarine to corn. Mix beaten eggs and milk. Stir mixture into corn and pour into a 1½ quart greased baking dish. Bake at 350 degrees for 35 minutes.

Yield: 8 servings

CORN PUDDING SUPREME

- **1 8–ounce package softened cream cheese**
- **2 beaten eggs**
- **⅓ cup sugar**
- **1 8½–ounce package cornbread/muffin mix**
- **1 16½–ounce can cream style corn**
- **2⅓ cups sweet corn**
- **1 cup milk**
- **2 tablespoons melted butter or margarine**
- **1 teaspoon salt**
- **½ teaspoon ground nutmeg**

In a mixing bowl, blend cream cheese, eggs and sugar. Add remaining ingredients and mix well. Pour into a 2 quart baking dish. Bake at 350 degrees for 45–50 minutes or until set.

Yield: 12–16 servings

Note: Equally delicious made with fresh, canned or frozen corn.

 *A grasshopper's jaws work like a pair of pliers.*

TEX-MEX CASSEROLE

- **3 cups cooked white rice**
- **1 10-ounce package frozen whole kernel corn**
- **1 clove finely chopped garlic**
- **⅓ cup sliced green onion**
- **1½ cups milk**
- **1 teaspoon chili powder**
- **½ teaspoon liquid red pepper seasoning**
- **½ teaspoon salt**
- **¼ teaspoon pepper**
- **2 cups shredded sharp Cheddar cheese (divided use)**
- **1 large thinly sliced tomato**

Preheat oven to 350 degrees. Grease a 2 quart baking dish. Thaw corn. Mix first nine ingredients and 1½ cups shredded cheese. Pour into dish. Arrange tomato slices on top, overlapping slightly. Bake at 350 degrees for 30–45 minutes. Sprinkle with remaining ½ cup cheese for last 5 minutes of baking time. Let stand 10 minutes before serving.

Yield: 8 servings

GREEN BEAN BAKE

- **2–3 14½-ounce cans drained whole green beans**
- **¼ cup milk**
- **1 8-ounce can drained and sliced water chestnuts**
- **1 10¾-ounce can cream of mushroom soup**
- **¼ teaspoon pepper**
- **1 2.8-ounce can French fried onion rings**

Gently mix first 5 ingredients and ½ can onion rings. Bake in uncovered 1 quart glass baking dish at 350 degrees for 30 minutes. Top with remaining ½ can of onion rings for the last 5 minutes of baking. Double for 9x13 inch dish.

Yield: 4–6 servings

GARLIC BUTTERED GREEN BEANS

- **1 pound fresh or frozen green beans**
- **½ cup sliced fresh mushrooms**
- **4 tablespoons butter**
- **2–3 teaspoons onion powder**
- **1 teaspoon garlic powder**
- **salt and pepper to taste**

Cover green beans with water and cook until tender. In a skillet, sauté mushrooms in butter until tender; add onion powder and garlic powder. Drain beans; add to skillet and toss. Season with salt and pepper.

Yield: 6 servings

GREEN BEAN BUNDLES

2 14½-ounce cans whole green beans
8–10 bacon slices
⅓ cup butter
⅓ cup brown sugar
1 teaspoon garlic salt

Put 12–14 green beans in a bundle. Wrap bundles with ½ slice bacon. Overlap bacon on bottom side and put in a greased baking dish. Melt butter. Add brown sugar and garlic salt and stir until completely smooth. Spoon sauce over each bundle. If doubling sauce, do not double garlic salt, add just a dash more. Bake uncovered at 350 degrees for 30–40 minutes.

Yield: 6–8 servings

CHEESE GRITS

3 beaten eggs
1 teaspoon salt
1 teaspoon savory salt
2 teaspoons Tabasco
1 teaspoon paprika
1½ cups quick grits
6 cups boiling water
¾ pound grated Cheddar cheese
¾ cup margarine

Beat together eggs, salts, Tabasco and paprika. Set aside. Prepare grits according to package instructions, cooling no longer that 3 minutes. Mix cheese and margarine into hot grits. Add egg mixture and blend well. Pour into lightly buttered baking dish. Bake at 300 degrees for 45 minutes or until lightly browned.

Yield: 8–10 servings

BAKED ONION RINGS

1 large onion
4 cups crushed cornflakes
1 teaspoon seasoned salt
2 teaspoons sugar
1 teaspoon paprika
2 eggs
vegetable cooking spray

Cut onions into thick slices and separate into rings. Combine cereal, seasoned salt, sugar and paprika. Beat eggs until stiff. Dip rings into beaten eggs and then into crumb mixture. Place on cookie sheet that has been sprayed with vegetable spray. Repeat until all rings are coated. Bake at 350 degrees for 15 minutes.

Yield: 4 servings

POTLUCK BLACKEYED PEAS

- ¼ pound diced bacon
- 2 cups chopped celery
- 2 cups chopped green pepper
- 2 16-ounce cans tomatoes
- 2 16-ounce cans blackeyed peas
- 2 cups chopped onion

Sauté bacon with celery, bell pepper and onion. Add tomatoes and peas. Simmer 30 to 40 minutes. Serve in soup bowls.

Yield: 6-8 servings

Note: Delicious served with Texas cornbread.

MILLION DOLLAR POTATOES

- 6 medium-large baking potatoes
- ½ cup softened margarine
- 2 cups shredded Cheddar cheese (divided use)
- 1 cup sour cream
- ¼ cup milk
- ½ teaspoon salt
- ¼ teaspoon pepper
- ¼ cup chopped chives
- 2 tablespoons Parmesan cheese

Wash, dry and oil potatoes. Bake at 400 degrees 1 hour or until done. Let cool to touch. Cut in half. Scoop out pulp leaving, shells intact. Combine pulp, margarine, 1 cup shredded cheese, sour cream, milk, salt and pepper; mix until smooth. Add more milk if necessary. Add chives and Parmesan cheese. Stuff potato shells. Place on cookie sheet and bake covered at 350 degrees for 10 minutes. Sprinkle with remaining shredded cheese; bake uncovered 10 minutes.

Yield: 6 servings

POTATOES ROMANOFF

- 2 teaspoons salt
- 2 cups creamed cottage cheese
- 1 cup sour cream
- ¼ cup minced green onions
- 1 small clove crushed garlic
- 5 cups cubed cooked potatoes
- ½ cup grated Monterey Jack cheese
- 1 teaspoon paprika

Mix first six ingredients. Pour into a greased 3 quart baking dish. Top with cheese and paprika. Bake at 350 degrees for 40 minutes.

Yield: 8 servings

POTATOES WITH SOUR CREAM SAUCE

- **6 medium new potatoes**
- **¼ cup butter**
- **1 10¾-ounce can cream of chicken soup**
- **1 cup sour cream**
- **⅓ cup chopped green onions**
- **1½ cups grated Cheddar cheese (divided use)**
- **¾ cup crushed cornflakes**

Boil potatoes with skin on. When cool, skin and cut into pieces. Heat and blend butter and soup. Add sour cream, onions and ¾ cup grated cheese. Mix well; pour into a 2 quart buttered baking dish. Add crushed cornflake crumbs on top and sprinkle remainder of grated cheese over crumbs. Bake at 350 degrees for 45 minutes.

Yield: 6 servings

MAKE-AHEAD MASHED POTATOES

- **8-10 peeled potatoes**
- **8 ounces softened cream cheese**
- **1 cup sour cream**
- **2 tablespoons chopped chives**
- **4 tablespoons butter or margarine**
- **salt and pepper**

Quarter potatoes; cover with water; boil 10 to 15 minutes or until soft when speared in the center. Drain well. Whip hot potatoes with cream cheese and sour cream. Continue beating until fluffy and smooth. Add chives, salt and pepper to taste. Place in 9x13 inch baking dish. Dot with butter; cover with foil and refrigerate. When ready to serve, bake covered at 350 degrees for 15 minutes. Uncover; continue baking until crusty on top.

Yield: 10 servings

POTATO FANS

- **4 medium unpeeled baking potatoes**
- **4 tablespoons softened butter or margarine**
- **1 1-ounce package dry ranch dressing mix**
- **salt and pepper to taste**

Wash potatoes; cut into ¼ inch slices across potatoes; do not cut all the way through. Mix dry dressing into butter; spread generously between each slice and over outside of potato. Bake uncovered at 400 degrees for 50 minutes or until done.

Yield: 4 servings

Note: Any dry dressing mix is delicious; potatoes may be peeled.

HASH BROWN CASSEROLE

- **1 chopped medium onion**
- **½ cup chopped green pepper**
- **½ stick butter or margarine**
- **1 cup sour cream**
- **1 10¾-ounce can cream of mushroom, celery or chicken soup**
- **1 cup shredded Cheddar cheese**
- **1 16-ounce package thawed, frozen hash brown potatoes**
- **1 cup crushed cornflakes, potato chips or bread crumbs**

Sauté onion and pepper in margarine. Combine all ingredients but potatoes and cornflakes and mix well. Add potatoes and mix well. Pour into greased 2 quart baking dish. Top with crushed cornflakes, potato chips or bread crumbs. Bake at 350 degrees for 55–60 minutes or until bubbly and browned.

Yield: 6–8 servings

The wolf spider spins a silk cocoon for her eggs which she carries in her jaws until the eggs hatch.

WHOOPEE POTATOES

- **2 16-ounce packages frozen hash brown potatoes**
- **2 cups half and half**
- **2 cups grated American cheese**
- **1 stick margarine or butter**
- **½ tablespoon salt**
- **2 8-ounce cartons sour cream**
- **8 slices crisp fried bacon**

Thaw potatoes; place in a 9x13 inch baking dish. In microwave, melt margarine, cheese and half and half. Pour over potatoes. Bake at 350 degrees for 60–70 minutes. Mix in sour cream and crumbled bacon and bake additional 15 minutes. Sprinkle grated cheese on top and bake 5 minutes.

Yield: 8 servings.

TUNA STUFFED POTATOES

8 medium baking potatoes
1 12-ounce can drained tuna
2½ cups mayonnaise
1½ cups grated Cheddar cheese
¾ cup finely chopped green pepper
½ cup chopped pimento
¾ cup chopped onions

Bake or microwave potatoes until done. Mix remaining ingredients. Salt and pepper to taste. Cut potatoes in half and scoop out pulp. Combine mixture with pulp and stuff potato shells. Bake at 375 degrees for 10–15 minutes.

Yield: 8 servings

SWEET POTATO SOUFFLÉ

2 29-ounce cans yams or sweet potatoes
1½ cups sugar
2 eggs
6 tablespoons melted margarine or butter
½ cup milk
⅔ teaspoon nutmeg
⅔ teaspoon cinnamon

Drain and mash sweet potatoes. Mix all ingredients well; pour into a 9x13 inch baking dish. Bake at 400 degrees for 20–30 minutes or until set.

Yield: 12 servings

SWEET POTATO SUPREME

3 large sweet potatoes
½ cup melted butter or margarine
½ cup sugar
⅓ cup milk
1 teaspoon vanilla
2 eggs

TOPPING:
1 cup light brown sugar
1 cup chopped pecans
⅓ cup flour
⅓ cup melted butter or margarine

Peel potatoes and cut into thin slices. Cover with water and boil 15–20 minutes or until tender. Whip with electric beater and remove any strings. Add butter and sugar to warm potatoes and continue mixing. Add milk, vanilla and eggs. Mix well. Pour into buttered 9x13 inch baking dish. Mix pecan topping ingredients; sprinkle on top of casserole. Bake at 350 degrees for 30–35 minutes.

Yield: 8–10 servings

JALAPEÑO SPINACH

- 2 10-ounce packages chopped frozen spinach
- 4 tablespoons butter or margarine
- 2 tablespoons flour
- 2 tablespoons chopped onions
- ½ cup evaporated milk
- ½ cup vegetable liquid from defrosted spinach
- ¾ teaspoon celery salt
- ¾ teaspoon garlic salt
- 1 6-ounce roll jalapeño cheese
- 1 teaspoon Worcestershire sauce
- buttered bread crumbs

Cook spinach according to directions on package. Drain and reserve liquid. Melt butter in saucepan over low heat. Add flour, stirring until blended; add onions and cook until soft. Add liquids slowly, stirring constantly; cook until smooth and thick. Add seasonings. Cut cheese into small pieces; stir into mixture until melted. Combine with cooked spinach. Put into 9x13 inch baking dish; top with buttered bread crumbs. Bake at 350 degrees for 45 minutes.

Yield: 8 servings

SHELLS WITH SPINACH AND RICOTTA

- 2 teaspoons canola oil
- 2 tablespoons chopped onion
- 1 10-ounce package drained frozen spinach
- ½ cup chicken broth
- 1 cup ricotta cheese
- ½ cup 2% milk
- 2 tablespoons grated Parmesan cheese (divided use)
- 6 ounces drained and cooked medium pasta shells
- 1 dash nutmeg
- salt and pepper to taste

Preheat oven to 425 degrees. Spray an 8 inch baking dish with cooking spray. In large skillet, heat oil, add onion and sauté for two minutes or until onion is translucent. Add spinach and sauté two minutes; add broth and salt and pepper to taste. Cook two more minutes and transfer to a large bowl. Add ricotta and milk to spinach mixture and stir well. Add nutmeg, one tablespoon of cheese and pasta shells. Transfer mixture to prepared baking dish. Sprinkle with remaining cheese. Bake 10 minutes, then place under broiler to brown lightly.

Yield: 6 servings

SPINACH/ARTICHOKE CASSEROLE

- **¾ cup softened butter or margarine**
- **1 8–ounce package cream cheese**
- **2 10–ounce packages frozen chopped spinach**
- **1 8–ounce can sliced water chestnuts**
- **1 14–ounce can water packed artichoke hearts**
- **1 large chopped onion**
- **¼ teaspoon garlic powder**
- **1½ tablespoons Worcestershire sauce**
- **bread crumbs**
- **Parmesan cheese**
- **salt and pepper to taste**

Defrost spinach and squeeze out water. Cream butter and cream cheese. Add sliced water chestnuts and spinach. Add seasonings and adjust to taste. Placed sliced artichoke hearts in bottom of 1½ quart baking dish sprayed with vegetable spray. Top with spinach mixture. Sprinkle bread crumbs and Parmesan cheese on top. Bake uncovered at 350 degrees for 30–40 minutes or until bubbly.

Yield: 8–10 servings

SPINACH STRATA

- **1 16–ounce package seasoned, crushed croutons**
- **½ cup melted margarine or butter**
- **½ cup Parmesan cheese**
- **2 10–ounce packages chopped spinach**
- **2 cups cottage cheese**
- **8 ounces shredded Monterey Jack cheese**
- **6 eggs**
- **½ cup chopped onion**
- **2 cloves garlic**
- **4 tablespoons sour cream**
- **¼ teaspoon nutmeg**
- **salt and pepper to taste**

Put croutons in 9x13 inch glass baking dish. Pour melted butter over crumbs. Thaw and drain spinach. Whisk eggs lightly and add all ingredients except spinach. Mix well and fold in spinach. Pour over crumb mixture. Bake at 350 degrees 35 minutes or until set. Let stand several minutes before serving.

Yield: 12 servings

SPINACH/ONION CASSEROLE

2 10-ounce packages frozen chopped spinach
1 10¾-ounce can cream of mushroom soup
1 egg yolk
1 egg white
1 3-ounce package cream cheese
1 2.8-ounce can onion rings
shredded Parmesan cheese

Heat spinach and drain well. In large saucepan, heat soup and cream cheese and stir until cheese is melted. Add beaten egg yolk to mixture and stir in spinach. Beat egg white until stiff and fold into spinach mixture. Sprinkle Parmesan cheese over mixture and top with onion rings. Bake at 350 degrees for 15 minutes or until bubbly.

Yield: 6–8 servings

SQUASH AND CARROT MEDLEY

6 medium grated zucchini squash
3 medium grated carrots
3 medium grated yellow squash
6 tablespoons butter or margarine
1 minced garlic clove
Parmesan cheese
salt and pepper to taste

Place squash on tea towel and wring out excess moisture. Melt butter in large Dutch oven. Add garlic and cook one minute over low heat. Add vegetables and cook 10 minutes, stirring occasionally. Add salt, pepper and Parmesan cheese.

Yield: 8 servings

LIGHT AND HEALTHY SQUASH CASSEROLE

3–4 medium yellow squash
3 egg beaters
¼ cup chopped onion
½ cup skim milk
1 roll crushed lightly salted Ritz crackers
3 ounces grated fat-free Cheddar cheese
salt and pepper to taste

Slice squash in ¼ inch rounds, steam slightly and drain. Put steamed squash in bottom of baking dish. Mix with egg beaters. Add onion and milk. Layer crackers on squash mixture. Bake at 350 degrees for 30 minutes. Add layer of cheese and bake 5 minutes or until melted.

Yield: 6 servings

CHEESY SQUASH

12 medium yellow squash
6 bacon slices
3 beaten eggs
¾ cup chopped onion
1½ cups shredded Cheddar cheese
1½ tablespoons Worcestershire sauce
salt and pepper to taste

Wash and slice squash in unpeeled ¼–inch rounds. Cook in small amount of boiling water until tender. Drain well and mash with potato masher. Cook bacon until crisp. Remove bacon and crumble. Sauté onion in bacon drippings. Add all ingredients and stir well. Spoon into lightly greased 1½ quart baking dish. Bake at 350 degrees for 30 minutes.

Yield: 6–8 servings

SAFFRON RICE

2 tablespoons olive oil
2 tablespoons butter or margarine
¼ teaspoon crumbled saffron
1 tablespoon boiling water
3 cups water
1½ teaspoons salt
1½ cups regular uncooked white rice

Blend oil with butter in a medium size saucepan over medium heat stirring occasionally. Mix saffron with boiling water and allow to stand a few minutes. Add 3 cups water to butter mixture and bring to a boil. Add saffron, water and rice. When mixture returns to boil, reduce heat, cover and simmer for 15–20 minutes until liquid is absorbed. Rinse in colander with cold water and separate rice with a fork. Place covered colander over hot water until rice is fluffy and grains stand alone.

Yield: 10 servings

The ruby-throated hummingbird has approximately 940 feathers.

LAYERED SQUASH CASSEROLE

- 6 cups diced yellow or zucchini squash
- 1 cup shredded carrots
- ¼ cup chopped onion
- 1 10¾-ounce can condensed cream of chicken soup
- 1 cup sour cream
- 1 8-ounce package herb seasoned stuffing
- ½ cup melted butter or margarine

Cover squash, carrots and onion with water and boil for 5 minutes, then drain. Combine chicken soup and sour cream. Fold the drained squash, carrots and onions into the soup and sour cream mixture. Combine stuffing mix with melted butter. Spread half the stuffing in the bottom of a 9x13 inch baking dish. Spoon vegetable mixture over the top. Sprinkle the remaining stuffing over vegetables. Bake at 350 degrees for 30 minutes.

Yield: 8–10 servings

TOMATO AND ARTICHOKE BAKE

- 2 14-ounce cans drained artichoke hearts
- 2 28-ounce cans drained tomatoes
- 1 cup chopped green onions with tops
- 4 tablespoons melted butter or margarine
- 2 tablespoons sugar
- 1 teaspoon dried basil
- Parmesan cheese
- salt and pepper to taste

Rinse artichokes with water and drain. Cut drained artichokes and tomatoes into quarters. Sauté green onions and tops in butter until tender. Stir in artichoke hearts, tomatoes and remaining ingredients. Pour into lightly oiled 3 quart glass baking dish. Bake uncovered at 350 degrees for 10–15 minutes or until heated through. Remove from oven and sprinkle with Parmesan cheese.

Yield: 10–12 servings

TOMATOES ROCKEFELLER

1 10–ounce package cut frozen spinach
1 minced garlic clove
¼ cup finely chopped green onions
½ cup butter or margarine
1 cup Italian–style bread crumbs
¼ cup grated Parmesan cheese
¼ teaspoon cayenne pepper
¼ teaspoon thyme
½ teaspoon black pepper
2 beaten eggs
6 large tomatoes

Cook spinach according to directions. Add garlic, onion and butter to hot spinach. Stir in next 5 ingredients. Add beaten eggs. Slice tomatoes into ½ inch slices. Using a large spoon, heap spinach mixture on top of each tomato slice. Top spinach with Parmesan cheese. Bake on greased cookie sheet at 325 degrees approximately 20 minutes.

Yield: 24–30 slices

BETH'S SONORA CASSEROLE

SAUCE:
2 cups tomato sauce
¼ teaspoon cumin
1½ teaspoons chili powder
¼ teaspoon cayenne pepper
1 tablespoon white vinegar
¼ teaspoon garlic powder
salt to taste

ZUCCHINI MIXTURE:
6 corn tortillas
3 cups sliced zucchini
1 cup fresh or canned corn
1 4–ounce can chopped green chilies
2 cups shredded mozzarella cheese

Mix sauce first and let ingredients simmer while preparing tortillas and zucchini. Cut tortillas into strips. Boil or steam zucchini slices. Add corn and green chilies. Layer tortillas, zucchini mixture, sauce and mozzarella in a 3 quart baking dish. Bake at 350 degrees for 20 minutes. Serve with diced shallots and sour cream.

Yield: 8–10 servings

ZUCCHINI TOMATO PIE

- 1 medium thinly sliced zucchini
- 2 large chopped tomatoes
- 1 medium thinly sliced onion
- salt and pepper to taste
- 1 tablespoon butter or margarine
- 1 cup grated Cheddar cheese
- 6 slices crispy cooked and crumbled bacon
- ½ cup Italian bread crumbs

Butter a 10 inch round deep glass pie plate. Layer zucchini, tomatoes and onion. Sprinkle lightly with salt and pepper. Dot with butter and sprinkle with cheese and bacon. Repeat layers and top with bread crumbs. Bake covered at 400 degrees for 60 minutes. Remove cover last 20 minutes.

Yield: 6 servings

Hummingbirds can fly up, down, sideways, backwards and upside down.

MIXED VEGETABLE CASSEROLE

- 3 15–ounce cans drained mixed vegetables
- 1 cup chopped celery or water chestnuts
- 1 small finely chopped onion
- 1 cup mayonnaise
- 1 cup grated Cheddar cheese
- 1 cup crushed Ritz crackers
- 4 tablespoons melted butter or margarine

Mix vegetables, celery, onion, mayonnaise and cheese and place in 2 quart baking dish. Top with crushed crackers and melted butter. Bake at 350 degrees for 35 minutes or until bubbly.

Yield: 10–12 servings

Sweet Cart

APPLESAUCE CAKE

1 16–ounce can applesauce
3 teaspoons baking soda
1 cup margarine (2 sticks, not whipped or lite) or butter
2¼ cups dark brown sugar
4 cups all purpose flour (divided use)
1 cup chopped pecans or walnuts
½ pound golden raisins
¼ teaspoon salt
2½ teaspoons cinnamon
1 teaspoon cloves
2 teaspoons orange or lemon peel

GLAZE:
1 cup confectioners sugar
1 lemon (squeezed for juice) or 3 tablespoons undiluted frozen orange juice

Heat applesauce until it continuously bubbles in a 3 quart saucepan. Add soda to the very hot applesauce when it is removed from the stove. Stir in margarine melted. Add brown sugar and mix until dissolved and blended. To 3 cups of flour, add the spices and salt. Gradually add to the contents of the pot, mixing thoroughly. To the remaining 1 cup of flour, stir in the pecans and raisins and add to the applesauce mixture. Turn into a well greased and floured angel food cake pan. Bake for 2 hours at 300 degrees. Test cake: an inserted toothpick or cake tester will come out clean when removed. Cool in angel food pan for approximately 10 minutes before removing. Glaze.

Yield: 12 servings

Note: This can be baked in a 9x13 inch cake pan, but the baking time is approximately 1 hour. Glaze flat cake immediately when removed from oven.

CREAMY APPLE SQUARES

1 box yellow cake mix (non–pudding)
½ cup margarine
4–5 thinly sliced apples
1 egg
1 cup sour cream
¼ cup brown sugar
½ teaspoon cinnamon

Combine mix and margarine until crumbly. Reserve ⅔ cup for top. Press remaining mixture in a 9x13 inch baking pan. Arrange the sliced apples over the bottom crust. Blend sour cream and egg, and spread over the apples. To the reserve mix, blend in sugar and cinnamon, and sprinkle over the top. Bake for 30 minutes in a 350 degree oven.

Yield: 10 servings

APPLE PIE CAKE

- **2 cups flour**
- **2 cups sugar**
- **½ cup vegetable oil**
- **2 eggs**
- **2 teaspoons cinnamon**
- **2 teaspoons baking soda**
- **1 teaspoon salt**
- **1 16–ounce can apple pie filling**

Combine all ingredients except pie filling in a large bowl, and blend well. Stir in the can of pie filling, and pour into a greased and floured 9x13 inch baking pan. Bake 1 hour at 350 degrees. Cool and frost.

FROSTING:

- **1½ cups powdered sugar**
- **2 3–ounce packages softened cream cheese**
- **5 tablespoons margarine**
- **1 teaspoon vanilla**

Combine ingredients and mix to spreading consistency.

Yield: 12 servings

BLACK RUSSIAN CAKE

- **1 box yellow cake mix**
- **½ cup sugar**
- **1 6–ounce package instant chocolate pudding**
- **1 cup vegetable oil**
- **4 eggs**
- **¾ cup water**
- **¼ cup Kahlua**
- **¼ cup vodka**

Blend all ingredients; mix until batter is fluffy. Bake in greased and floured bundt or tube pan at 350 degrees for 55–60 minutes or until cake tester comes out clean. Cool 15 minutes and remove from pan.

GLAZE:

- **½ cup powdered sugar**
- **¼ cup Kahlua**

Mix until smooth. Punch holes into slightly cooled cake; drizzle glaze over cake.

Yield: 10–12 servings

CHOCOLATE COLA CAKE

- **2 cups sifted all purpose flour**
- **2 cups granulated sugar**
- **1 teaspoon baking soda**
- **1 cup butter or margarine**
- **3 heaping tablespoons cocoa**
- **1 cup of cola beverage**
- **3 eggs**
- **½ cup of buttermilk**
- **1 teaspoon vanilla**
- **1½ cups of miniature marshmallows**
- **1 cup chopped walnuts or pecans**

Combine sifted flour, sugar and soda and mix well with electric mixer. Set aside. Melt butter or margarine in microwave oven for 1 minute and stir in cocoa. Microwave for 1 minute: add cola. With the mixer on low, gradually add butter, cocoa, and cola mix to the flour sugar mixture. Add buttermilk, eggs and vanilla and mix until blended. Do not beat. Pour into a greased 9x13 inch baking pan. Bake at 350 degrees for 30 to 35 minutes or until a wooden pick inserted in center comes out clean. As soon as cake is removed from oven, sprinkle marshmallows over the top. Do not remove cake from pan. Sprinkle chopped nuts over this. Quickly spoon frosting over marshmallow nut topping while cake is still warm and spread.

COLA FROSTING:

- **½ cup margarine**
- **4 tablespoons of cocoa**
- **1 16-ounce package of powdered sugar**
- **¼ cup of cola (1 or 2 tablespoons of cola may be added if needed to make frosting easily spreadable)**
- **1 teaspoon vanilla**

Melt margarine in saucepan and add remaining ingredients. Cook slowly until all is blended.

Yield: 12 servings

Note: Do not use diet cola or whipped or low fat margarine.

Eagle feathers are held together by more than 350,000 tiny hooks which make the feather incredibly strong.

MILKY WAY CAKE

- **1½ cups plus 2 tablespoons butter or margarine**
- **1 cup finely chopped pecans**
- **4 3.63–ounce Milky Way bars**
- **2½ cups flour**
- **¾ teaspoon baking soda**
- **¼ teaspoon salt**
- **1½ cups granulated sugar**
- **4 eggs**
- **1 teaspoon vanilla**
- **1½ cups buttermilk**

Grease a 10 inch bundt pan with 2 tablespoons of butter. Tilt and add sprinkle chopped nuts to cover sides. Leave loose nuts in bottom. Melt candy and ½ cup butter over medium heat, and let cool slightly. Mix flour, baking soda, and salt in a small bowl and set aside. In a large mixing bowl beat 1 cup butter and sugar. Add eggs one at time, beating after each addition. Add vanilla and candy mixture. Add flour alternately with buttermilk, beating after each addition until well blended. Pour into prepared bundt pan, and bake 1 hour or until tester inserted in center comes out clean. Cool in pan on rack for 30 minutes. Invert on rack and frost.

FROSTING:

- **1 3.63–ounce Milk Way bar**
- **½ cup butter or margarine**
- **2 cups powdered sugar**
- **1–2 tablespoons milk**

Over low heat melt candy and butter. Beat in powdered sugar. Add milk to desired consistency. Frost cake.

Yield: 10–12 servings

CHERRY PIE CAKE

- **2 15–ounce cans red pie cherries and juice**
- **1 cup granulated sugar**
- **2 tablespoons tapioca**
- **2 tablespoons white corn syrup**
- **1 box yellow cake mix**
- **1 cup chopped pecans**
- **¾ cup soft margarine**

Grease a 9x13 inch baking dish and pour in cherries. Be sure cherries are evenly spread over bottom of the dish. Sprinkle sugar over the cherries and sprinkle tapioca evenly over the mixture. Drizzle white corn syrup over the top. Cover with the dry yellow cake mix. Sprinkle with 1 cup chopped pecans. Cover top of mixture evenly with margarine and spread so cake will be wet all over. Bake 60 minutes at 350 degrees. This can be served slightly warm with ice cream or whipped cream.

Yield: 15–20 squares

BANANA NUT CAKE

- **1 cup margarine**
- **2 cups granulated sugar**
- **2½ cups flour**
- **1 teaspoon baking soda**
- **1 teaspoon baking powder**
- **½ teaspoon salt**
- **½ cup buttermilk**
- **4 egg whites**
- **6 mashed bananas**
- **1 cup chopped pecans**

In a large mixing bowl cream margarine and sugar. Sift together flour, soda, baking powder and salt, and add to creamed mixture. Stir in buttermilk, egg whites, mashed bananas and pecans. Turn into a greased and floured 9x13 inch baking pan. Bake for 35 minutes in a preheated 350 degree oven. Cool in pan.

ICING:

- **1 8–ounce package cream cheese**
- **½ cup margarine**
- **1 (16–ounce) box confectioners sugar**

Mix at room temperature and ice.

Yield: 10–12 servings

ALMOND COCONUT CAKE

- **1½ cups all purpose flour**
- **½ cup yellow cornmeal**
- **2 teaspoons baking powder**
- **½ teaspoon salt**
- **1 cup sugar**
- **¼ cup softened butter or margarine**
- **½ teaspoon almond extract**
- **⅔ cup milk**
- **3 large egg whites**
- **½ cup + 2 tablespoons shredded coconut**
- **2 tablespoons sliced natural almonds**

Preheat oven to 350 degrees. Lightly coat an 8 inch springform pan with vegetable spray. Combine flour, cornmeal, baking powder and salt. In another bowl, beat sugar and butter at medium speed until combined. Beat in almond extract. Add flour mixture alternately with milk, beginning and ending with dry ingredients until blended. In a clean bowl, beat egg whites until stiff. Fold gently into batter mixture with rubber spatula, then fold in ½ cup coconut. Spoon batter evenly into prepared pan; sprinkle with remaining 2 tablespoons coconut and almonds. Bake 45 to 50 minutes until lightly browned and toothpick inserted in center comes out clean. Cool pan on wire rack 10 minutes. Remove side of pan. Serve warm or at room temperature.

Yield: 8 servings

COCONUT SPICE CAKE

- **1 cup granulated sugar**
- **1 cup brown sugar**
- **1 cup vegetable oil**
- **2 eggs**
- **2½ cups all purpose flour**
- **1 teaspoon baking soda**
- **½ teaspoon salt**
- **1 teaspoon cinnamon**
- **1 teaspoon nutmeg**
- **1 cup buttermilk**
- **1 teaspoon vanilla**
- **1 cup shredded coconut**
- **1 cup chopped pecans**

In a large mixing bowl combine sugars and oil. Add eggs and blend. Mix flour, baking soda, salt and spices together. Add this to the mixture alternating with buttermilk. Beat until well blended. Stir in coconut and nuts. Pour into a greased 9x13 inch baking dish and bake for 35 minutes at 350 degrees.

FROSTING:

- **½ cup butter or margarine**
- **1 8–ounce package softened cream cheese**
- **1 16–ounce box confectioners sugar**

Cream butter, sugar and cream cheese until fluffy. Add confectioners sugar and beat until smooth. Stir in pecans and frost cake. Sprinkle coconut on top.

Yield: 10 servings

DUMP CAKE

- **1 20–ounce can crushed pineapple**
- **3–4 tablespoons sugar**
- **1 21–ounce can cherry or apple pie filling**
- **1 box white cake mix**
- **¾ cup margarine**
- **1 cup chopped pecans**

Butter a 9x13 inch baking dish. Dump can of crushed pineapple with its juice over the bottom. Sprinkle lightly with sugar. Dump can of pie filling on top of pineapple. Cover with the dry white cake mix. Dot with the softened small pieces of margarine. Top with chopped pecans. Do not mix any of this. Bake in a 300 degree oven for 45 minutes or until brown.

Yield: 10 servings

CRÈME DE MENTHE CAKE

1 box white cake mix
6 tablespoons green crème de menthe (divided)
1 16–ounce jar thick fudge sauce
1 8–ounce container whipped topping

Mix white cake mix according to directions on the box; stir 3 tablespoons of crème de menthe into the batter. Pour into a greased 9x13 inch baking pan. Bake according to box instructions. Cool. Spread thick fudge sauce over top of cake. Stir 3 tablespoons of crème de menthe into tub of whipped topping, and spread over the fudge topping. Keep in the refrigerator until ready to serve.

Yield: 12 servings

KEY LIME CAKE

1 box lemon cake mix
1 3–ounce box lemon instant pudding mix
½ cup vegetable oil
1 cup water
3 eggs
2 tablespoons Key lime juice
⅛ teaspoon green food coloring

Mix all ingredients and pour into a greased and floured 9x13 inch baking pan. Bake for 30 minutes at 350 degrees. Glaze.

GLAZE:
1 cup confectioners sugar
⅓ cup lime juice

Mix and put ½ glaze on cake when it is removed from the oven and the other half after it has cooled.

Yield: 12 servings

KUPUA CAKE

1 box yellow pudding cake mix
1 14–ounce package coconut
1 8½–ounce can cream of coconut
1 9–ounce container non–dairy whipped topping

Prepare cake as directed on package. Blend in 1 cup of coconut and pour in a 9x13 inch glass baking dish. Bake as directed in a 350 degree oven for 30 minutes. When the cake is done, pierce holes in hot cake with a fork. Pour the cream of coconut over cake. After it has cooled, spread on whipped topping, and sprinkle with the remaining coconut.

Yield: 12 servings

NEAPOLITAN ICEBOX CAKE

- **1 small package strawberry gelatin**
- **1 box marble cake mix**
- **1 3–ounce package vanilla instant pudding**
- **1 cup milk**
- **1 teaspoon vanilla**
- **1 8–ounce container whipped topping**

Prepare gelatin using ¾ cup boiling water and ½ cup cold water. Set aside. Mix marble cake as directed. Pour into a 9x13 inch pan and bake according to instructions on cake box. Cool 20 to 25 minutes. Poke holes in cake about 1 inch apart, and pour in gelatin. Refrigerate while preparing topping. Thoroughly mix the instant vanilla pudding with milk and vanilla. Blend in the whipped topping (can use an electric mixer). Frost cake and refrigerate. Serve chilled.

Yield: 12 servings

PINEAPPLE SUPREME CAKE

- **1 box pineapple cake mix**
- **1 20–ounce can undrained crushed pineapple**
- **1 3–ounce package instant vanilla pudding**
- **1 8–ounce carton whipped topping**

Mix pineapple cake according to directions on box and pour into a 9x13 inch baking pan. Bake as instructed. Cool. For the topping add pineapple to dry pudding, and mix thoroughly. Blend in whipped topping and mix. Spread on top of cooled cake. Keep in refrigerator. Serve chilled.

Yield: 10–12 servings

POPPY SEED CAKE

- **1 box yellow butter cake mix**
- **½ cup granulated sugar**
- **½ cup poppy seeds**
- **¾ cup oil**
- **4 eggs**
- **1 8–ounce carton sour cream**

In an electric mixer, mix 1 box cake mix, sugar, poppy seeds, oil and eggs one at a time. Continue mixing and add sour cream. Turn in a greased and floured bundt pan. Bake for 1 hour in a 350 degree oven. Cool in pan for 10 minutes: remove by inverting.

Yield: 10–12 servings

POUND CAKE SUPREME

- 3 cups granulated sugar
- 1 cup softened butter or margarine
- 5 eggs
- 3 cups all purpose flour
- 1 teaspoon salt
- 1 cup buttermilk
- ¼ teaspoon baking soda
- 1 tablespoon hot water
- 1 tablespoon vanilla extract
- 1 tablespoon lemon extract
- 1 tablespoon orange extract
- 1 teaspoon almond extract

Cream sugar and butter or margarine until light and fluffy. Add eggs one at a time. Sift flour with salt. Add to sugar mixture alternating with buttermilk, and beat well. Dissolve soda in 1 tablespoon hot water and add to mixture along with flavorings. Continue beating until well blended. Pour into tube pan sprayed with vegetable cooking oil. Bake in 300 degree oven for 1½ hours or until inserted tester comes out clean.

Yield: 10–12 servings

PUMPKIN CAKE

- 2 cups all purpose flour
- 2 cups granulated sugar
- 3 teaspoons cinnamon
- 2 teaspoons baking soda
- 1 teaspoon salt
- 1½ cups oil
- 2 cups canned pumpkin
- 4 eggs

Blend dry ingredients with an electric mixer set on low. Add remaining ingredients and beat for 1 minute. Pour into a 10 inch greased and floured tube pan. Bake 1 hour at 325 degrees or until tester comes out clean. Let cool 20 minutes and turn onto plate, and glaze.

GLAZE:

- ½ pound confectioners sugar
- ¼ cup butter or margarine
- 1 3-ounce package softened cream cheese
- 1 teaspoon vanilla
- 2 tablespoons milk or cream
- whole pecans

Beat all ingredients until smooth and spoon over warm cake. Garnish with pecans.

Yield: 10–12 servings

PUMPKIN PIE CAKE

- **1 16–ounce can pumpkin**
- **1 12–ounce can evaporated milk**
- **3 eggs**
- **4 teaspoons pumpkin pie spice**
- **½ teaspoon salt**
- **1 cup granulated sugar**
- **1 yellow cake mix**
- **2 cups chopped pecans**
- **1½ cups melted butter**

Mix the first 6 ingredients together. Pour this mixture into a 9x13 inch pan. Sprinkle yellow cake mix over the top. Sprinkle chopped pecans over the cake mix. Drizzle melted butter over top. Bake in a preheated 350 degree oven for 1 hour or until tester comes out clean. Serve with a dollop of whipped cream seasoned with 1 teaspoon cinnamon. Sprinkle with nutmeg.

Yield: 10–12 servings

Note: Do not use a yellow cake mix with butter or pudding.

PUMPKIN SWIRL

- **3 large eggs**
- **1 cup granulated sugar**
- **⅔ cup canned pumpkin**
- **¾ cup biscuit mix**
- **2 teaspoons pumpkin pie spice**
- **1 cup chopped pecans**
- **2–3 tablespoons confectioners sugar**
- **1 8–ounce package softened cream cheese**
- **⅓ cup softened butter or margarine**
- **1 cup sifted confectioners sugar**
- **1 teaspoon vanilla extract**

Grease bottom and sides of a 15x10 inch jelly roll pan; line with wax paper and set aside. Beat eggs at high speed with an electric mixer until thickened. Gradually add sugar, beating until soft peaks form and sugar dissolves (2 to 4 minutes). Fold in pumpkin. Combine biscuit mix and spices; fold into pumpkin mixture and spread evenly into prepared pan. Sprinkle with chopped pecans. Bake at 375 degrees for 13 to 15 minutes. Sift 2 to 3 tablespoons confectioners sugar in a 15x10 inch rectangle on a cloth towel. When the cake is done immediately loosen from sides of pan, and turn out onto sugared towel. Peel off wax paper. Starting at narrow end, roll up cake and towel together; cool completely on a wire rack, seam side down.

Beat cream cheese and butter at medium speed with an electric mixer until creamy; add 1 cup confectioners sugar and vanilla, beating well. Unroll cake, spread with cream cheese mixture, and reroll without towel. Place on a serving plate, seam side down; chill at least 2 hours.

Yield: 12 servings

FORGOTTEN CAKE

8 egg whites
1½ cups of sugar
1 teaspoon cream of tartar
¼ teaspoon salt
1 teaspoon vanilla extract
1 8–ounce container Cool Whip
1 10–ounce package frozen raspberries or any fresh fruit

Beat egg whites lightly, using a slow setting on your mixer. Add the cream of tartar and salt. Beat until peaks form. Slowly add the sugar while continuing to beat. Lightly grease a 9x13 inch glass baking dish. When the sugar is dissolved and the egg whites are stiff put the mixture into the baking dish and place in a preheated 425 degree oven. Turn heat off, and let cake set in the oven overnight. Do not peak. The next morning spread cool whip over the top. Refrigerate at least four hours. Cut in squares and top with fruit.

Yield: 12 servings

RASPBERRY TRIFLE

1 3–ounce package vanilla pudding mix (not instant)
2 cups milk
1 teaspoon almond flavoring

Make pudding according to package directions, add flavoring and cool.

1 3–ounce package raspberry gelatin
1 10–ounce package frozen raspberries

Add 1 cup boiling water to gelatin mix. When partially cooled, add thawed raspberries. Save a few for garnish. Refrigerate until jelled.

1 angel food cake, cut in ¾ inch cubes

In a 1½–quart bowl alternate pudding and gelatin with cake cubes. Chill to set up, at least 4 hours.

TOPPING:
1 8–ounce tub of whipped topping
¼ teaspoon vanilla extract
½ cup slivered almonds

Before serving, spread whipped topping over mixture and garnish with raspberries and slivered almonds.

Yield: 8–10 servings

RASPBERRY CHOCOLATE TRUFFLE CAKE

- **1 box bittersweet chocolate plus one piece**
- **½ cup superfine sugar**
- **½ cup unsalted butter plus 6 tablespoons**
- **8 eggs**
- **1 10–ounce package frozen raspberries in syrup**
- **2 teaspoons Framboise (Chambord), optional**
- **2 pints vanilla ice cream**

Lightly oil an 8½ inch springform pan. Place bowl and beaters of electric mixer in freezer to chill for at least 30 minutes.

Melt chocolate and butter in double boiler over hot water (or in microwave) stirring occasionally, until smooth. Remove from heat and whisk in sugar. Let chocolate stand, stirring occasionally until sugar is completely dissolved, about 5 minutes. Whisk in one egg at a time. Pour ⅓ of chocolate mixture into prepared pan and freeze for a least 30 minutes. Cover remaining chocolate mixture with plastic wrap and set aside at room temperature.

In food processor or blender purée raspberries. Stir in Framboise. Place 1 pint of ice cream in the chilled bowl and beat until softened for about 15 seconds. Spread half of the ice–cream over frozen chocolate layer and freeze. Return bowl and beaters to freezer.

Pour half of remaining chocolate mixture over frozen ice cream layer and freeze. Beat remaining ice cream in chilled bowl to soften. Spread over chocolate layer and freeze. Pour remaining chocolate over top of cake. Cover and freeze overnight or at least 6 hours.

To unmold, soak kitchen towel in hot water, wring out and wrap around cake before removing side of pan. Do not remove cake from the bottom of the pan. Cover cake with plastic wrap and refrigerate for 1 hour before slicing.

Yield: 12 or more servings

The entire skeleton of a bald eagle weighs only a little more than half a pound.

CAPPUCCINO CHEESECAKE

CRUST:

1¼ cups graham cracker crumbs
¼ cup firmly packed dark brown sugar
1 teaspoon cinnamon
½ cup melted unsalted butter

Preheat oven to 375 degrees. In a bowl stir together all crust ingredients and press onto bottom of a 10 inch springform pan.

FILLING:

3 8-ounce packages softened cream cheese
1½ cups sugar
4 large eggs
⅓ cup strong brewed instant espresso

In a bowl with an electric mixer beat cream cheese and sugar until smooth. Beat in eggs, 1 at a time. Add cooled espresso and continue beating until smooth. Pour filling onto crust and bake cheesecake on a baking sheet in middle of oven for 35 minutes, or until center is barely set. Open oven door, pull rack out and allow cheesecake to cool in pan on rack. Chill, covered overnight. Remove side of pan and top cheesecake with whipped cream topping.

TOPPING:

1 cup well chilled heavy cream
¼ teaspoon cinnamon
¾ teaspoon unsweetened cocoa powder

In a bowl beat cream to stiff peaks. Sift cocoa powder and cinnamon over top.

Yield: 12 servings

As hummingbirds hover, their wings twist in the shape of a propeller and the wingtips move in a figure 8 to give perfect control.

GERMAN FRUIT CAKE (3 PRESERVE CAKE)

¾ cup butter or margarine
2 cups granulated sugar
4 eggs
3 cups sifted all purpose flour
½ teaspoon allspice
½ teaspoon cinnamon
½ teaspoon nutmeg
1 cup buttermilk
¾ teaspoon baking soda
⅔ cup cherry preserves
⅔ cup apricot preserves
⅔ cup pineapple preserves
1 cup chopped pecans
1 teaspoon vanilla

In a bowl with an electric mixer, cream butter and sugar until light. Add eggs and blend. Mix flour with spices. Dissolve soda in butter milk. Add dry ingredients and buttermilk alternately to creamed mixture; mixing well after each addition. Fold in preserves, pecans and vanilla. Bake in greased and floured tube pan at 325 degrees for 1½ hours. Cool pan for 15 minutes before removing cake.

Yield: 16 servings

Note: Very rich and very heavy, best for Thanksgiving and Christmas season.

PASTRY

FOR SINGLE CRUST:
1½ cups sifted all purpose flour
½ teaspoon salt
½ cup shortening
4–5 tablespoons cold water

FOR DOUBLE CRUST:
2 cups sifted all-purpose flour
1 teaspoon salt
⅔ cup shortening
5–7 tablespoons cold water

Sift together flour and salt. Cut in shortening with pastry blender until pieces are the size of small peas. Add water, a tablespoon at a time, blending with a fork until all mixture is moistened. Form into a ball and knead lightly on floured board. Form into a ball and roll to about ⅛ inch thick to desired size.

For baked pie shell, fit loosely into pie pan, prick bottom and sides with fork, and bake in 450 degree oven 10 to 12 minutes, or until golden brown.

For unbaked crust, do not prick pastry. Pour pie filling into crust and bake as directed in pie recipe.

MERINGUE SHELLS

4 egg whites
1 teaspoon ice water
¼ teaspoon cream of tartar
1 cup granulated sugar
½ teaspoon vanilla

Beat egg whites, water and cream of tartar until foamy. Gradually beat in sugar and vanilla. Beat until stiff peaks form and all sugar is dissolved. Line cookie sheet with brown paper. Drop heaping tablespoons of mixture onto paper. Using back of spoon, shape into shells. Bake at 275 degrees for 1 hour. Cool.

Yield: 6–8 servings

BROWNIE PIE

2 beaten eggs
1 cup granulated sugar
½ cup melted butter
1 teaspoon vanilla
⅔ cup all purpose flour
⅓ cup cocoa
¼ teaspoon salt
1 cup chocolate chips
½ cup nuts

Combine eggs, sugar, butter and vanilla. Stir together flour, cocoa and salt. Mix into butter mixture and stir in chocolate chips and nuts. Pour into lightly greased 9 inch pie plate. Bake at 350 degrees for 30 minutes or until set.

Yield: 6–8 servings

COCONUT CHESS PIE

½ cup milk
1½ cups grated coconut
¼ cup margarine
1 cup granulated sugar
3 eggs
1 teaspoon lemon juice
1 9 inch pie shell

Pour milk over coconut and set aside. Cream margarine and sugar together. Add eggs, one at a time, beating well after each. Stir in coconut mixture and lemon juice. Pour into pie shell and bake at 350 degrees for 30 minutes or until browned.

Yield: 8 servings

PINEAPPLE PECAN PIE

- **1 cup firmly packed brown sugar**
- **1 tablespoon all purpose flour**
- **3 eggs**
- **1 cup pineapple ice cream topping**
- **1 teaspoon vanilla extract**
- **4 tablespoons melted butter or margarine**
- **1 cup chopped pecans**
- **1 9 inch pie crust**

In a small bowl, combine the brown sugar and flour and mix well. Combine the eggs, pineapple topping, vanilla and melted butter. Beat until well mixed. Add brown sugar mixture and beat well. Stir in the pecans. Pour into pie crust and bake in a 350 degree oven for 1 hour, or until the filling is set and pecans are golden brown.

Yield: 8 servings

CHOCOLATE–RUM PECAN PIE

- **2 ounces unsweetened chocolate**
- **2 ounces sweet butter**
- **4 lightly beaten eggs**
- **1¼ cups dark corn syrup**
- **1 cup granulated sugar**
- **1 teaspoon vanilla extract**
- **2 tablespoons dark rum**
- **1 cup pecan pieces**
- **1 9 inch pie shell**

Melt chocolate and butter together. Beat eggs into chocolate. Add sugar and corn syrup and beat well. Stir in vanilla, rum, and pecans. Pour into pie shell and bake in a 350 degree oven for 50 minutes. Remove from oven and cool. Serve at room temperature, topped with a dollop of whipped cream.

Yield: 8 servings

CARAMEL PECAN PIE

- **28 caramels (slightly less than a 1-pound package)**
- **¼ cup water**
- **¼ cup margarine**
- **¾ cup granulated sugar**
- **¼ teaspoon salt**
- **½ teaspoon vanilla extract**
- **2 beaten eggs**
- **1 cup chopped pecans**
- **1 9 inch pie crust**

Unwrap caramels and place in top of double boiler with water and margarine. Stir occasionally until melted and smooth. In separate bowl combine sugar, salt, vanilla and beaten eggs. Gradually add caramel mixture, mixing well. Stir in pecans. Pour into pie shell and bake in a 350 degree oven for 30 minutes.

Yield: 8 servings

DATE–NUT PIE

- 12 finely chopped pitted dates
- 1 cup finely chopped pecans
- 1 cup sugar
- 12 finely crushed Premium crackers
- ½ teaspoon baking powder
- 3 stiffly beaten egg whites
- 1 teaspoon almond or vanilla extract
- 1 cup whipping cream
- ⅛ cup sugar

Mix chopped dates, pecans, sugar, crackers and baking powder. Blend well. Beat egg whites until stiff and lace with almond or vanilla extract. Fold into date mixture. Place mixture in a 9 inch greased pie plate. Bake in preheated 350 degree oven for 30 minutes or until light brown. Let cool before cutting. Top cooled pie with sweetened whipped cream.

Yield: 8 servings

 *Ants touch their feelers together to communicate with each other.*

TOLL HOUSE PIE

- 2 eggs
- ½ cup all-purpose flour
- ½ cup granulated sugar
- ½ cup brown sugar
- ¼ cup melted butter or margarine
- ½ cup chocolate chips
- ½ cup chopped walnuts or pecans
- 1 cup whipping cream or ice cream

Beat eggs until foamy. Add flour and sugars, beating until well blended. Blend in melted butter or margarine. Carefully stir in chocolate chips and nuts. Pour into greased 9 inch pie plate. Bake in a preheated 325 degree oven for 30 minutes or until set and light golden. Can be served hot or cool, topped with sweetened whipped cream or ice cream.

Yield: 8 servings

BLUEBERRY DEEP–DISH PIE

¼ cup flour
1 cup sugar
¼ teaspoon nutmeg
5 cups blueberries
2 teaspoons grated lemon rind
2 tablespoons butter
double crust pastry

Blend together flour, sugar and nutmeg in large bowl. Gently fold blueberries and lemon rind into flour mixture. Roll out ½ pastry and fit into a deep–dish pie pan. Pour in blueberry mixture. Dot with butter. Roll out the remaining pastry and place over blueberry mixture, crimping edges. Brush with cold milk and sprinkle granulated sugar over crust. Bake at 425 degrees for 20 minutes. Reduce heat to 350 degrees and bake 35 minutes longer or until top crust is golden brown.

Yield: 10 servings

MACADAMIA NUT PIE

4 eggs
⅔ cup (minus 1 tablespoon) sugar
1 cup light corn syrup
2 tablespoons melted butter
1½ cups chopped macadamia nuts
2 teaspoons vanilla extract
1 9 inch pie shell

In a bowl, beat eggs with sugar. Add corn syrup, butter, nuts and vanilla. Blend well. Pour into pie shell and bake on bottom rack of oven at 325 degrees for 50 minutes. Serve with whipped cream, if desired. May be prepared a day ahead. Freezes well after cooling.

Yield: 6–8 servings

MILLIONAIRE PIE

1 can drained crushed pineapple
1 can sweetened condensed milk
¼ cup lemon juice
1 8 ounce container non–dairy whipped topping
1 cup chopped pecans or walnuts
2 graham cracker crusts

Mix all ingredients and pour into two graham cracker crusts. Chill 24 hours.

Yield: 12–16 servings

MACAROON STRAWBERRY PIE

1⅓ cups sweetened coconut
½ cup chopped almonds
⅓ cup granulated sugar
2 tablespoons all purpose flour
⅛ teaspoon salt
2 egg whites
½ teaspoon almond extract
1½ cups non-dairy whipped topping
1½ cups sliced ripe strawberries

Mix first five ingredients together in bowl. Stir in egg whites and almond extract until blended. Grease a cookie sheet and line with aluminum foil. Spread macaroon mixture into a 9 inch circle on prepared pan. Bake in 350 degree oven for 15–20 minutes or until lightly browned. Cool on rack. Remove to serving plate. Spread whipped topping over top of macaroon, leaving a slight edge showing. Arrange sliced strawberries over topping.

Yield: 8 servings

BEST EVER CHOCOLATE PIE

1½ cups granulated sugar
2 heaping tablespoons all purpose flour
3 tablespoons cocoa
1 12-ounce can evaporated milk
4 egg yolks (reserve whites for meringue)
½ cup margarine
1 teaspoon vanilla extract
⅛ teaspoon salt
1 baked 9 inch pie shell

Mix together sugar, flour, cocoa, milk and beaten egg yolks, beating well. Cook over medium heat until mixture boils and thickens, stirring constantly. Remove from heat and add margarine, vanilla and salt. Beat well and pour into baked pie shell. Top with meringue. Brown 15 minutes in a 350 degree oven.

MERINGUE:
4 egg whites
¼ teaspoon cream of tartar
6 tablespoons granulated sugar
½ teaspoon vanilla extract

Beat egg whites. Add cream of tartar and vanilla extract. Add sugar gradually, 1 tablespoon at a time, until meringue is stiff.

Yield: 8 servings

FRESH STRAWBERRY PIE

GLAZE:

- **3 cups sliced fresh strawberries**
- **1 cup sugar**
- **3 tablespoons cornstarch**

Mix strawberries and sugar only and let stand for 30 minutes. Stir in cornstarch and cook over medium heat until very thick and clear. Set aside until cool.

- **1 baked and cooled 10 inch pie shell**
- **1 8 ounce package room temperature cream cheese**
- **½ cup sugar**
- **2 tablespoons fresh lemon juice**
- **1 teaspoon grated lemon rind**
- **2 tablespoons milk or cream**
- **1 pint sliced fresh strawberries**
- **½ pint whipping cream**

Mix cream cheese, sugar, lemon juice, rind, cream (or milk) and beat until consistency of whipped cream. Line cool pie shell with cream cheese mixture. Cover cream cheese mixture with 1 pint sliced strawberries. Cover with cooled glaze. Refrigerate until well chilled. Before serving, top with sweetened whipped cream.

Yield: 8 servings

KAHLÚA PIE

- **1 9 inch baked and cooled deep-dish pie crust**
- **1 cup softened butter or margarine**
- **1½ cups granulated sugar**
- **2 squares melted unsweetened chocolate**
- **4 eggs**
- **¼ cup Kahlúa**
- **½ pint whipping cream**
- **2 tablespoons granulated sugar**
- **¼ cup toasted sliced or slivered almonds**

In a large mixing bowl beat together butter, sugar and chocolate. Add eggs, one at a time, beating 3 minutes after each addition (for a total of 12 minutes). This is very important. Stir in Kahlúa. Pour into baked and cooled pie crust. In a small mixing bowl whip cream until stiff. Gradually add sugar toward end of beating. Spread on top of pie. Sprinkle with almonds. Chill for at least 4 to 6 hours.

Yield: 8–10 servings

Note: Very rich. Small servings are savored and appreciated. Recipe may be halved when using small crust.

GRASSHOPPER PIE

20 finely crushed chocolate creme-filled cookies
¼ cup melted butter
20 large marshmallows
½ cup milk
½ pint whipping cream
1½ ounces crème de menthe
1½ ounces crème de cacao

Make crust by combining cookies and melted butter. Press into 9 inch pie plate. Make filling by heating marshmallows in ½ cup milk until melted. Cool and add mixture of whipped cream, crème de menthe and crème de cacao. Put filling into pie crust and chill until set (about 4 hours).

Yield: 8 servings

VIENNESE APRICOT PIE

2 slightly beaten eggs
2 cups sour cream
1½ cups sugar
¼ cup plus ⅓ cup flour (divided use)
⅛ teaspoon nutmeg
½ teaspoon salt
4 drops almond extract
1½ cups dried apricots
1 10 inch pie shell
½ cup light brown sugar
¼ cup butter or margarine

Combine eggs, sour cream, sugar, ¼ cup flour, nutmeg, salt and almond extract. Beat well with rotary beater. Plump apricots; drain and cut into small pieces. Stir into egg mixture and pour into pie shell. Bake at 400 degrees for 25 minutes. Meanwhile, combine remaining ⅓ cup flour with light brown sugar. Mix well and cut in the butter until mixture resembles coarse crumbs. Remove pie from oven and sprinkle well with the crumbly mixture. Return pie to oven and continue baking for 20 to 25 minutes, or until the filling is set. Cool to room temperature or chill before serving. Garnish with whipped cream if desired.

Yield: 8 servings

The longest-lived animal is the tortoise of which one was recorded as being over 152 years old.

PEACHES AND CREAM PIE

6–8 peeled and sliced soft ripe peaches (or well drained 28 ounce can sliced peaches)
⅓ cup granulated sugar
⅔ cup granulated sugar
¼ cup flour
¼ teaspoon salt
½ pint whipping cream
½ teaspoon vanilla
¼ teaspoon almond extract
1 9 inch pie shell

In a bowl, sprinkle peeled and sliced peaches with ⅓ cup sugar. Set aside. Mix together ⅔ cup sugar, flour and salt. Add unwhipped cream and flavorings. Mix well. Put peaches in bottom of crust and pour cream mixture over peaches. Put pie on a cookie sheet in a 400 degree oven for about 40 minutes or until almost set in middle. Serve slightly warm.

Yield: 6–8 servings

COUSIN PAT'S PEACH TORTE

½ cup soft butter
½ cup granulated sugar
¼ teaspoon vanilla
¾ cup flour
⅔ cup chopped pecans
1 8–ounce package cream cheese
¼ cup granulated sugar
1 egg
½ teaspoon vanilla

TOPPING:
1 teaspoon granulated sugar
1 teaspoon cinnamon
1 29–ounce can drained and cut up peaches

Cream butter, sugar and vanilla. Add flour and pecans and press into bottom and sides of jelly roll pan. Beat remaining ingredients and pour over crust. Arrange topping on cream cheese mixture. Bake at 450 degrees and bake 25 minutes or until cheese is set and crust is brown.

Yield: 8–10 servings

STRAWBERRY YOGURT TARTS

GRAHAM CRACKER CRUST:

- **1⅓ cups graham cracker crumbs**
- **⅓ cup melted margarine**
- **1 tablespoon granulated sugar**

Mix all ingredients and press into sides and bottom of 12 foil tart cups.

- **2 8-ounce packages strawberry yogurt**
- **½ cup mashed strawberries**
- **1 8-ounce container non-dairy whipped topping**
- **12 small graham cracker tart cups**
- **1 pint sliced fresh strawberries**

Fold yogurt and fruit into whipped topping. Spoon into tarts and freeze. Remove from freezer 30 minutes before serving and top with fresh strawberries.

Yield: 12 tarts

TRIPLE DELIGHT

- **2 tablespoons sugar**
- **½ cup softened margarine**
- **1 cup flour**
- **¾ cup chopped pecans**
- **1 8-ounce package softened cream cheese**
- **1 cup powdered sugar**
- **1 12-ounce container non-dairy whipped topping**
- **1 4.5-ounce package instant vanilla pudding mix**
- **1 4.5-ounce package instant lemon pudding mix**
- **3 cups milk**

Combine sugar, margarine, flour and ½ cup pecans and press into a 9x13 inch baking dish. Bake at 350 degrees for 20 minutes. Cool. Beat cream cheese, powdered sugar and 1 cup whipped topping together and spread on crust. Combine vanilla, pudding mixes and milk. Pour over cream cheese mixture. Spread remaining whipped topping on top and sprinkle with remaining ¼ cup pecans. Refrigerate or freeze until serving.

Yield: 20 servings

Note: Chocolate pudding mix can be used instead of lemon pudding mix.

FABULOUS AND EASY PEACH COBBLER

6–8 peeled and diced fresh peaches
¼ cup sugar
¼ cup water
1 cup flour
2 teaspoons baking powder
½ teaspoon salt
1 cup sugar
1 beaten egg
½ cup cold butter
1 cup finely chopped pecans (optional)

Place peaches in 9x13 inch baking dish. Sprinkle with ¼ cup sugar and ¼ cup water. Mix flour, baking powder, salt, 1 cup sugar and egg until crumbly. Chopped pecans may be added to flour mixture, if desired. Sprinkle over top of peaches and add ½ cup butter in thin slices over all. Bake in a 350 degree oven for 40 minutes.

Yield: 10–12 servings

Note: Two 29 ounce cans chopped sliced peaches can be substituted for fresh peaches. Reserve ¼ cup juice and sprinkle over peaches if needed. Omit ¼ cup sugar and ¼ cup water.

The fastest creature ever recorded is the spine-tailed swift at 106 mph.

APPLE CRISP

6 apples
½ cup water
½ cup red hots
¾ cup flour
½ cup butter
1 cup sugar

Pare, core and thinly slice apples. Fill greased 9x13 inch casserole with apples, water and red hots. Blend dry ingredients until crumbly and spread mixture over apples. Bake in 350 degree oven for 75 minutes or until apples are tender and crust is brown.

Yield: 8 servings

CHOCOLATE SOUFFLÉ

12 ounces semi-sweet chocolate chips
1½ teaspoons almond or vanilla extract
⅛ teaspoon salt
1½ cups whipping cream
6 egg yolks
2 egg whites

Heat whipping cream to boiling. Combine chocolate, almond or vanilla extract and salt in a blender or food processor. Mix for 30 seconds. Add boiling cream and mix another 30 seconds or more until chocolate melts. Add egg yolks. Mix 5 seconds. Transfer to a bowl and allow to cool. Beat 2 egg whites until stiff and fold gently into chocolate mixture. Cover bowl with plastic wrap and refrigerate 2–3 hours. After soufflé has set, garnish with additional whipped cream with sugar and extract added and toasted almonds. Keep refrigerated until serving time.

Yield: 6 servings or 20 demitasse size servings

MOUSSE AU CHOCOLAT

¾ cup softened butter
1½ cups sugar
½ teaspoon almond extract
1 tablespoon brandy
3 separated eggs
½ pound semi-sweet chocolate or chocolate chips
¼ cup toasted slivered almonds
1½ cups heavy whipping cream

Beat butter until creamy and blend in sugar, almond extract, brandy and egg yolks. Melt chocolate and add to butter mixture. Fold in stiffly beaten egg whites and whipped cream. Pour into individual serving dishes and garnish with whipped cream, toasted almonds and/or chocolate curls. Refrigerate until well set.

Yield: 10–12 servings

FLAN

- **4 well beaten eggs**
- **1 14–ounce can condensed milk**
- **1 can whole homogenized milk**
- **1 tablespoon vanilla**
- **⅛ teaspoon salt**
- **6 tablespoons sugar**

Mix all ingredients except sugar and set aside. Melt sugar in a heavy skillet until caramel colored. Be careful not to burn. Pour into 8 inch mold or dish. When cool, pour in egg mixture. Bake in a pan of hot water in a 350 degree oven for 1 hour and 15 minutes.

Yield: 6 servings

SWEDISH APPLE PUDDING

- **½ cup butter**
- **2 cups granulated sugar**
- **2 large eggs**
- **2 cups flour**
- **2 teaspoons baking soda**
- **2 teaspoons cinnamon**
- **½ teaspoon salt**
- **4 cups finely chopped peeled apples**
- **1 cup chopped pecans**

Cream together butter, sugar and eggs. Mix together flour, soda, cinnamon and salt and add to butter mixture. Stir in apples. Pour batter into two 9 inch square pans. Sprinkle top of each pudding with ½ cup chopped pecans. Bake in a 350 degree oven for 40 minutes. Cut in squares and top with warm sauce.

SAUCE:

- **½ cup butter**
- **½ cup cream**
- **1 cup brown sugar**
- **1 teaspoon vanilla**

Stir until mixture comes just to a boil. Keep warm until ready to serve.

Yield: 12–16 servings

 *Golden eagles can live to be 45 years old.*

DIVINE! BREAD PUDDING

1 loaf French bread
3½ cups milk
2 cups sugar
1 teaspoon vanilla
½ cup golden or dark raisins
1 8 ounce can undrained crushed pineapple
4 lightly beaten eggs
dash nutmeg or cinnamon

Tear bread into 5–6 cups bite–size pieces. Pour milk over bread and allow bread to absorb milk. Mix sugar, vanilla, raisins, pineapple, eggs and nutmeg or cinnamon. Add egg mixture to bread mixture and gently fold until blended. Pour into 9x13 inch glass baking dish that has been sprayed with cooking spray. Bake 55–60 minutes in a 350 degree oven. Serve with custard sauce or whiskey sauce.

CUSTARD SAUCE:
2 eggs
2 tablespoons sugar
dash salt
1 cup scalded milk
½ teaspoon vanilla
½ teaspoon grated lemon rind

Combine eggs, sugar and salt in top of a double boiler, beating well. Gradually stir about ½ cup milk into egg mixture. Add remaining milk and stir constantly over hot water until mixture thickens, about 15 minutes. Cool slightly and add vanilla and lemon rind. Serve warm.

WHISKEY SAUCE:
½ cup butter
1 cup sugar
½ teaspoon cinnamon
½ teaspoon lemon juice
½ teaspoon vanilla
2 tablespoons whiskey

Cook over low heat until butter is melted and sugar dissolved. Remove from heat and stir in vanilla and bourbon. Serve warm.

Yield: 12–15 servings

 *Beavers usually work at night and decide where to place logs by listening to the flow of the water.*

PEACH BREAD PUDDING

1¼ cups plus 1 tablespoon sugar
6 tablespoons melted butter or margarine
3 cups milk
6 whole eggs or 2 whole eggs and 8 egg whites
1 pound loaf French Vienna bread
1 teaspoon cinnamon
2 29 ounce cans drained and sliced peaches (divided use)

Cube bread and place in jelly roll pan. Drizzle butter over bread and toss. Bake in a 350 degree oven 15–20 minutes or until light brown. Let cool. Purée 1 can peaches in food processor. Cut other can of peaches into smaller pieces. Reduce oven to 275 degrees. Butter a 10x15 inch glass pan and sprinkle with 1 tablespoon sugar. Beat eggs, milk and ¾ cup sugar. Add puréed and chopped peaches. Add bread and pour into prepared pan. Combine the remaining sugar and cinnamon and sprinkle over top. Bake 60 to 75 minutes covered. Uncover for last 10–15 minutes if a browner crust is desired.

BRANDY SAUCE:
2 teaspoons cornstarch
2 cups milk
1 teaspoon vanilla
6 egg yolks
6 tablespoons sugar
4 tablespoons brandy

Dissolve cornstarch in 4 tablespoons milk. Scald remaining milk and vanilla in heavy small saucepan. Whisk cornstarch mixture into milk. Whisk yolks and sugar in bowl until thick and pale. Gradually whisk in milk mixture. Whisk back into saucepan and stir over medium heat until sauce thickens enough to leave path on back of spoon when finger is drawn across; do not boil. Remove from heat and stir in brandy.

Yield: 20 servings

APRICOT SQUARES

⅔ cup dried apricots
½ cup butter
1 cup flour
2 egg yolks
½ cup coconut
½ teaspoon baking powder
⅔ cup water
¼ cup sugar
½ cup flour
¼ teaspoon salt
¾ cup brown sugar

ICING:
¼ cup butter
2 cups confectioners sugar
rind and juice of lemon

Preheat oven to 300 degrees. Cut apricots into small pieces and simmer in water for 15 minutes or until all water is absorbed. Mix butter, sugar, and 1 cup flour and press into a 9 inch square cake pan; bake for 15 minutes. Remove from oven and increase oven to 325 degrees. Beat 2 egg yolks and combine with brown sugar, coconut, ½ cup flour, salt, baking powder, apricots, and any remaining cooking water. Spread mixture on crust and bake for 25 minutes. Meanwhile combine butter, confectioners sugar, and lemon. Spread on cooled squares.

Yield: 25 squares

BROWNIE CARROT SQUARES

1 19.8–ounce package fudge brownie mix
4 large eggs
2 cups grated carrots
1½ cups mayonnaise
1 cup sugar
1 teaspoon ground cinnamon
1 teaspoon vanilla extract
1 cup chopped pecans

Combine first 7 ingredients in a large mixing bowl; beat at low speed with an electric mixer about 2 minutes. Stir in pecans. Pour batter into a greased 9x13 inch pan; bake at 350 degrees for 50 to 55 minutes or until a wooden pick inserted into the center comes out clean. Cool in pan on a wire rack. Cut into squares. Dust cake with powdered sugar, if desired.

Yield: 15–18 servings

BUTTERMILK BROWNIES

- 2 cups flour
- 2 cups sugar
- 4 tablespoon cocoa
- 1 cup water
- ¼ cup margarine
- ½ cup salad oil
- ½ cup buttermilk
- 1 teaspoon soda
- 2 eggs

FROSTING:

- ½ cup margarine
- ¼ cup cocoa
- ⅓ cup buttermilk
- 1 pound box powdered sugar
- 1 teaspoon vanilla
- ½ cup chopped nuts

Sift flour, sugar and cocoa together. Add boiling water, margarine and oil. Add to dry ingredients. Beat until creamy. Beat buttermilk, soda and eggs together and add to other mixture. Bake on 10x15 inch jelly roll pan at 350 degrees for 20 minutes. Boil margarine, cocoa, buttermilk, powdered sugar, vanilla and nuts, beat and let set, beat again. Cool brownies before frosting.

Yield: 16–20 servings

CARAMEL BROWNIES

- 1 14–ounce package caramels
- ⅔ cup evaporated milk, divided use
- 1 package Swiss chocolate cake mix
- ¾ cup margarine
- 1 cup chopped nuts
- 1 6–ounce package chocolate chips

Melt caramels in ⅓ cup evaporated milk. Combine cake mix with margarine and ⅓ cup evaporated milk and nuts. Mix and pour scant ½ mixture in greased 9x13 inch pan. Pat to cover bottom and bake in 350 degree oven for 6 minutes. Pour caramel mixture over this and sprinkle with chocolate chips. Spoon remainder of batter on top and smooth. Bake at 350 degrees for 15 minutes.

Yield: 24 servings

MOCHA BROWNIES

- 2¼ cups packed brown sugar
- ¾ cup salted margarine
- 2 tablespoons instant coffee powder
- 1 tablespoon hot water
- 2 eggs
- 2 tablespoons vanilla extract
- 2 cups flour
- 2 teaspoons baking powder
- ½ teaspoon salt
- 1 cup chopped pecans
- 1 cup semisweet chocolate chips

In medium saucepan, combine brown sugar and margarine over medium low heat. Cook until margarine is melted. Dissolve coffee powder in hot water and stir into margarine mixture. Cool to room temperature. Beat eggs and vanilla into cooled mixture. Sift together flour, baking powder and salt. Stir into mixture. Stir in pecans and chocolate chips. Grease 7x11 inch baking pan. Spread evenly into prepared pan. Bake at 350 degrees for 30 minutes or until lightly browned. Do not over bake. Cool and cut into 2 inch squares.

Yield: 20 servings

VI'S BLONDE BROWNIES

- ½ cup melted margarine
- 1½ cups light brown sugar
- 2 eggs
- 1 teaspoon vanilla
- 1 cup flour
- 1 teaspoon baking powder
- ½ teaspoon salt
- ¾ cup semi-sweet chocolate chips
- 1 cup chopped pecans, optional

Combine butter or margarine with brown sugar, eggs and vanilla and set aside. Mix flour, baking powder and salt; fold into mixture. Add chocolate chips and pecans. Pour into an 8x8 inch square oven proof dish, sprayed with cooking oil. Bake at 350 degrees for 30–35 minutes. Let cool and dust with powdered sugar.

Yield: 16–20 servings

EASY CHEWY PECAN SQUARES

1¼ cups biscuit baking mix
3 eggs
1½ cups brown sugar
¾ cup chopped pecans

Blend all ingredients and spread into a greased 9x13 inch baking pan. Bake at 350 degrees for 20 to 25 minutes. Cool and sprinkle top with powdered sugar.

Yield: 24 servings

SALTED NUT BARS

3 cups flour
1½ cups packed brown sugar
1 teaspoon salt
1 cup butter
1 12–ounce can mixed nuts
½ cup white corn syrup
2 tablespoons butter
1 tablespoon water
1 6–ounce package butterscotch chips

Combine first 4 ingredients and press into a 12x18 inch jelly roll pan. Bake at 350 degrees for 10 minutes. Sprinkle nuts over crust. Combine next 4 ingredients in small saucepan and boil 2 minutes, pour mixture over nuts. Bake at 350 degrees for 10–12 minutes or until golden brown. Cool and cut into squares.

Yield: 24 servings

DATE–NUT SQUARES

¾ cup chopped dates
¾ cup raisins
1 cup water
¼ cup butter
1 teaspoon baking soda
1 cup flour
¼ teaspoon salt
½ teaspoon cinnamon
¼ teaspoon nutmeg
2 eggs
3 tablespoons frozen unsweetened apple juice (thawed)
½ cup chopped pecans

Simmer dates and raisins in water for 5 minutes. Stir in butter, cool. Mix remaining ingredients together. Stir in cooled fruit mixture. Pour into greased 9x13 inch pan. Bake at 350 degrees for 15–20 minutes. Cool, cut into 2 inch squares.

Yield: 16–20 squares

PINEAPPLE SQUARES

- 1 cup sugar
- 2 cups flour
- 1½ teaspoons soda
- ½ teaspoon salt
- 1 15¼-ounce can crushed pineapple
- 2 eggs

ICING:

- 1 cup sugar
- ½ cup margarine
- 1 5-ounce can evaporated milk
- 1 cup chopped pecans
- 1 3½-ounce can coconut
- 1 teaspoon vanilla

Mix first 6 ingredients with spoon and pour into a 9x13 inch pan that has been greased and floured. Bake at 350 degrees for 25–30 minutes. For icing mix sugar, margarine and evaporated milk in saucepan. Boil 4 minutes, stirring constantly. Remove from heat and add pecans, coconut and vanilla. The icing should be ready to pour on the cake when it is done.

Yield: 15 squares

SEVEN LAYER COOKIES

- ½ cup butter
- 1 cup crushed graham crackers, (24 crackers)
- 1 cup shredded angel flake coconut
- 1 6-ounce package chocolate bits
- 1 6-ounce package butterscotch bits
- 1 14-ounce can condensed milk
- 1 cup chopped pecans

Melt butter and pour in an 8x11 inch pan. Sprinkle crushed graham cracker crumbs evenly over melted butter. Sprinkle coconut over cracker crumbs evenly; then chocolate bits; then butterscotch bits; using a tablespoon drizzle condensed milk evenly over all. Sprinkle chopped pecans over all and press down gently. Bake at 350 degrees for 30 minutes. Cool in pan and cut into small squares or bars. Store in refrigerator in a covered container. Serve at room temperature.

Yield: 12 servings

JACKIE'S OOEY GOOEY SQUARES

1 package yellow butter cake mix
1 beaten egg
½ cup soft margarine
1 16-ounce box powdered sugar
1 teaspoon vanilla
2 beaten eggs
1 8-ounce package cream cheese

Mix first 3 ingredients and press into a 9x13 inch glass baking dish. Blend next 4 ingredients for 5 minutes with mixer. Pour over first mixture and bake 350 degrees for 30–40 minutes. Do not over bake.

Yield: 48 small squares

ALMOND SANDIES

1 cup granulated sugar
1 cup softened butter or margarine
1 teaspoon almond extract
1 egg
2¼ cups flour
½ teaspoon baking soda
2 cups coarsely chopped slivered almonds, divided use

In mixing bowl, cream sugar, butter, egg, and almond extract until light and fluffy. Mix 1 cup almonds and baking soda into flour and add to mixture, blending well. Drop by teaspoon onto ungreased cookie sheet. Flatten dough and sprinkle cookies with remaining chopped almonds. Bake at 350 degrees for 10–12 minutes or until slightly brown on edges.

Yield: 5 or 6 dozen

POLISH FILLED TEA COOKIES

1 cup butter
½ cup granulated sugar
¼ teaspoon vanilla
2 cups flour
¼ teaspoon salt
1 cup chopped almonds
1 cup seedless raspberry jam
powdered sugar

Cream butter and sugar, add vanilla, flour, salt and almonds. Roll on lightly floured board, as thin as possible. Cut with biscuit cutter. Bake at 375 degrees for 8–10 minutes on a greased cookie sheet. When cool make sandwiches by spreading jam on one cookie and topping with another. Dust with powdered sugar. These are best the same day they are made. Especially nice for Christmas or Valentines.

Yield: 2 dozen

CASHEW AND COCONUT COOKIES

- 2¼ cups all purpose flour
- ½ teaspoon baking soda
- ¼ teaspoon salt
- ¾ cup packed light brown sugar
- ½ cup white sugar
- ¾ cup softened salted butter
- 2 large eggs
- 2 teaspoons vanilla extract
- ¾ cup sweetened shredded coconut, divided use
- 1 cup chopped raw salted cashews
- 1½ cups chopped dates

In a medium bowl combine flour, soda and salt. Mix well with a wire whisk and set aside. In a medium bowl combine sugars with an electric mixer at medium speed. Add butter and mix to form a grainy paste. Add eggs and vanilla; beat until smooth. Add flour mixture, ½ cup coconut, cashews and dates. Blend at low speed just until combined. Do not over mix. Drop by rounded tablespoon onto ungreased baking sheets, 2 inches apart. Sprinkle tops lightly with reserved coconut. Bake at 300 degrees for 23 to 25 minutes or until bottoms turn golden brown.

Yield: 2½ dozen

GREAT GRANNIE'S SUGAR COOKIES

- 1 cup butter
- 1 cup sugar
- 1 cup powdered sugar
- 1 cup oil
- 2 eggs
- 1 teaspoon vanilla
- 4 cups flour
- 1 teaspoon baking soda
- 1 teaspoon cream of tartar
- ½ teaspoon lemon zest

Cream butter, sugar, eggs and oil. Add vanilla and rest of ingredients. Do not stir more than necessary. Refrigerate dough for 4 hours. Grease cookie sheets. Scoop dough into inch balls and place on cookie sheets. Use flat bottom glass dipped in sugar to slightly flatten balls. Bake at 350 degrees for 13–15 minutes.

Yield: 5 dozen

HOLIDAY SUGAR COOKIES

- **1 cup butter**
- **2 cups sugar**
- **2 eggs**
- **2 teaspoons vanilla**
- **4 cups flour**
- **2 teaspoons baking powder**
- **½ teaspoon salt**

Cream butter and sugar. Add eggs, mixing well. Add vanilla. Mix in flour, sifted with salt and baking powder, kneading toward the last if necessary. Refrigerate 1 hour. Roll out about ¼ inch thick onto waxed paper sprinkled with half sugar and half flour. Use turkey or appropriate cookie cutters. Bake at 375 degrees for 10–15 minutes or until lightly browned.

Yield: 3 dozen

OATMEAL COCOA CHIPPERS

- **1½ cups all purpose flour**
- **½ cup cocoa**
- **2 teaspoons baking soda**
- **½ teaspoon salt**
- **1 cup softened butter or margarine**
- **1 cup firmly packed brown sugar**
- **½ cup sugar**
- **1 teaspoon vanilla extract**
- **2 eggs**
- **1 12-ounce package semi-sweet chocolate chips**
- **2 cups oatmeal (quick or old fashioned)**
- **1 cup chopped walnuts**

In a small bowl combine flour, cocoa, baking soda and salt; set aside. In large mixing bowl, combine margarine, brown sugar, sugar and vanilla extract. Beat until creamy. Add eggs one at a time, beating well after each addition. Gradually beat in flour mixture. Stir in oatmeal, chocolate chips and walnuts. Drop by slightly rounded measuring tablespoons onto ungreased cookie sheet. Bake at 350 degrees for 12–13 minutes for crisp cookies. Let stand 2 minutes before removing from cookie sheet.

Yield: 5 dozen

CHOCOLATE CHIP COOKIES

- **1½ cups brown sugar**
- **½ cup sugar**
- **1 cup plus 2 teaspoons softened butter**
- **2 eggs**
- **2 teaspoons vanilla extract**
- **1½ cups flour**
- **1 teaspoon baking soda**
- **1 teaspoon baking powder**
- **1 teaspoon salt**
- **½ cup grapenut cereal**
- **2¼ cups old fashioned oats**
- **1 cup chopped pecans**
- **1 12–ounce package semi sweet chocolate chips**

Cream sugars with butter. Beat in eggs then vanilla. Sift flour with baking soda, salt and baking powder and add to creamed mixture, mixing well. Stir in cereal, oats, pecans and chocolate chips. Drop by teaspoon onto baking sheets. Bake at 350 degrees for 5 to 8 minutes or until brown. May be prepared ahead. Freezes well.

Yield: 7 dozen

ANN'S SOFT RAISIN COOKIES

- **1 cup water**
- **2 cups raisins**
- **1 cup shortening**
- **1¾ cups sugar**
- **2 lightly beaten eggs**
- **1 teaspoon vanilla extract**
- **3½ cups all purpose flour**
- **1 teaspoon baking powder**
- **1 teaspoon baking soda**
- **1 teaspoon salt**
- **½ teaspoon ground cinnamon**
- **½ teaspoon ground nutmeg**
- **½ cup chopped walnuts**

Combine raisins and water in a small saucepan; bring to a boil. Cook for 3 minutes; remove from the heat and let cool (do not drain). In a mixing bowl, cream shortening; gradually add sugar. Add eggs and vanilla. Combine dry ingredients; gradually add to creamed mixture and blend thoroughly. Stir in nuts and raisins. Using teaspoon drop 2 inches apart on greased baking sheets. Bake at 350 degrees for 12–14 minutes.

Yield: 6 dozen

DELICIOUS FEED A CROWD COOKIES

- **1 cup white sugar**
- **1 cup brown sugar**
- **1 cup margarine**
- **1 cup oil**
- **1 egg**
- **1 teaspoon vanilla**
- **3½ cups all purpose flour**
- **1 teaspoon baking soda**
- **1 teaspoon cream of tartar**
- **1 teaspoon salt**
- **1 cup rice krispies**
- **1 cup coconut**
- **1 cup oatmeal**
- **½ cup chopped nuts**

In a large mixing bowl, blend sugars, oil, margarine, egg and vanilla. Add flour, salt, soda and cream of tartar, add remaining ingredients. Drop by small spoonfuls and press down with fork onto greased cookie sheet. Bake at 350 degrees for 12–15 minutes.

Yield: 100 cookies

MEXICAN PRALINE COOKIES

- **1 cup firmly packed light brown sugar**
- **1 cup softened unsalted butter**
- **1 large egg yolk**
- **½ teaspoon cinnamon**
- **⅛ teaspoon salt**
- **2 cups flour**
- **1 cup finely chopped pecans, toasted (see note)**
- **2 tablespoons confectioners sugar**

In a bowl, cream sugar and butter until smooth. Mix in egg yolk, cinnamon and salt. Add flour and mix well. Add chopped pecans and mix until just blended. Take a tablespoon of dough and roll into a ball. Place on ungreased baking sheet 2 inches apart. Bake at 350 degrees, for about 22 minutes or until edges begin to turn brown. Cool completely on wire rack, sprinkle tops with confectioners sugar.

Yield: 3 dozen

Note: To toast pecans, preheat oven to 350 degrees. Spread pecans in single layer on baking sheet. Bake on middle rack until color deepens, 7 to 10 minutes. Watch carefully so they do not burn. Toasted pecans can be frozen for several months.

FRUIT CAKE COOKIES

- ½ cup butter
- ½ cup brown sugar
- ¼ cup grape jelly
- 2 eggs
- ½ teaspoon nutmeg
- ½ teaspoon cloves
- ½ teaspoon cinnamon
- ½ teaspoon allspice
- 1½ cups flour
- ½ teaspoon soda
- 1½ tablespoons red wine
- 1 cup pecan pieces
- ½ pound chopped candied pineapple
- ½ pound chopped candied cherries
- 1 pound white raisins

Cream butter and sugar. Add eggs and jelly. Dissolve soda in wine. Add to egg mixture. Dredge fruit and nuts in half the flour and spice mixture. Add remaining flour gradually to mix. Fold in fruit. Drop from teaspoon onto greased cookie sheet. Bake at 300 degrees for 20 minutes.

Yield: 6 dozen

PECAN CLUSTERS

- 3 tablespoons butter
- 2 cups broken pecan pieces (do not chop)
- 1 pound almond bark

Melt butter on a jelly roll pan and cover with pecan pieces. Toast for 20 to 25 minutes, stirring every 10 minutes, being careful that they do not get too brown. Let cool. Break almond bark into small chunks and microwave in a glass bowl for 90 seconds. Remove and stir well. Microwave 15 seconds more; remove and stir until all chunks are melted and mixture is creamy (if necessary return and microwave 15 seconds more). Stir in cooled pecans and drop by teaspoon on wax paper. May be stored in an air tight container in freezer until needed.

Yield: 36–48 pieces

CINNAMON CANDY PECANS

- 1 egg white
- 1 tablespoon rum
- ½ cup sugar
- ¼ teaspoon salt
- 1 tablespoon cinnamon
- 1 pound chopped pecans

Beat egg white with rum until frothy. Combine dry ingredients and add to egg mixture. Stir to blend, add pecans. Toss to coat. Spread on cookie sheet. Bake 225 degrees for 1 hour. When cool, break apart.

Yield: 1 pound

ALMOND BUTTER CRUNCH

½ cup butter
½ cup sugar
1 tablespoon water
1 tablespoon light corn syrup
1 cup lightly toasted and chopped fine almonds
1 4–ounce block German sweet chocolate

Melt butter in quart saucepan. Add sugar, water and corn syrup. Stir constantly until sugar melts. Cook over low heat until candy thermometer reaches 190 degrees, takes about 15 minutes. Quickly remove from heat and add half of almonds. Using a spatula, spread mixture thinly onto a buttered cookie sheet. Slide spatula under candy to loosen as it cools. Melt chocolates, spread half over cooled candy and sprinkle with half of remaining nuts. When set, turn over and repeat with remaining chocolate and nuts. Break into pieces. Store in air tight container. If you ice only one side, you can double butter, sugar, water and corn syrup and make twice as much.

Yield: 2 dozen

CASHEW BRITTLE

1 cup sugar
1 cup water
1 cup light corn syrup
2 cups cashews
1 teaspoon vanilla
½ teaspoon baking soda

Combine sugar, water and corn syrup in heavy–bottomed 3 quart saucepan. Cook, stirring occasionally, over medium–high heat until temperature registers 275 degrees on candy thermometer, or soft–crack stage, about 20 minutes (mixture forms pliable strands when drizzled from a metal spoon). Stir in the cashews. Continue cooking, stirring occasionally to prevent the nuts from scorching, until the temperature reaches 305 degrees, or hard–crack stage, 5 to 7 minutes longer (mixture will be amber–colored and, when dropped into ice water and removed and bent, will snap). Remove the saucepan from the heat. Quickly stir in the vanilla and the baking soda. With a wooden spoon, quickly scrape hot brittle mixture onto a large greased cookie sheet. Working fast with back of wooden spoon, push brittle mixture to the edges of cookie sheet. Before brittle cools, stretch it out thinly by lifting and pulling from edges with two forks.

Yield: 1½ pounds

MICROWAVE QUICK CARAMEL CORN

3 quarts of popped corn

CARAMEL SAUCE:

1 cup brown sugar
½ cup margarine
¼ cup corn syrup
¼ teaspoon salt
½ teaspoon soda

Boil the brown sugar, butter, syrup and salt in a 2 quart glass measuring cup for 2 minutes on medium. Don't let it burn! Remove and stir in ½ teaspoon baking soda. Stir well; pour over the popped corn and spread in a 9x13 inch glass pan. Place in microwave and cook for 6–7 minutes, stirring every 2 minutes. Remove from the microwave and spread on waxed paper to cool. Store in covered container for crispness.

Yield: 3 quarts

SODA CRACKER CANDY

35–40 saltine crackers
1 cup butter
1 cup packed brown sugar
1½ cups semi–sweet chocolate chips
1½ cups coarsely chopped walnuts

Line a 10x15 baking pan with foil and coat with non–stick cooking spray. Place crackers in rows on foil. In saucepan, melt butter and brown sugar and bring to a boil. Boil 3 minutes. Pour over crackers and spread until crackers are completely covered. Bake 350 degrees for 5 minutes (crackers will float). Remove from oven. Turn off oven. Sprinkle chocolate chips and walnuts over crackers. Return to oven until chocolate melts (3–5 minutes). Press nuts into chocolate. Cut while warm.

Yield: 36 pieces

TOFFEE

1 large grated chocolate Hershey bar
1 cup butter
1 cup sugar
½ cup slivered almonds

Spread ½ of grated chocolate on cookie sheet. In heavy saucepan, melt butter and sugar together until a dark caramel color then add almonds. Spread over grated chocolate. Cover with other ½ of grated chocolate. Let cool and break into pieces. Store in air tight container.

Yield: 36 pieces

Luncheon Menus

Each year the Heard Museum Volunteer Guild sponsors two major fund-raisers benefiting the museum: a spring fashion show and a fall review. Just prior to each event, the Guild's Catering Committee gathers to select the menu. Members bring a wide variety of tempting options to a tasting. After everyone gets to sample and savor all the possibilities, a menu is chosen. Great care is taken that the meal will be as enticing to the eye as it is to the taste buds.

These menus, which have been used to serve over two hundred people per event, can be depended on to provide both a pretty presentation and a delicious luncheon.

Luncheon #1:

Ham Roll-ups

Sunshine Salad

Oriental Pea Salad

Strawberry Yogurt Tarts

Herbed Bread Sticks

Harvard Tea

Luncheon #2:

Party Chicken Salad

Peggy's Mystery Salad

Finger Sandwiches

Crystallized Dill Slices

Pineapple Supreme Cake

Harvard Tea

Luncheon #3:

Chicken Salad Crêpes

Parmesan Spinach Pasta

Salad de Albaricoque

Herbed Bread Sticks

Neapolitan Ice Box Cake

Harvard Tea

Luncheon #4:

Ham and Melon Kabobs with Mustard Sauce

Ashville Salad

Fruited Spinach Salad with Red Wine Vinaigrette

Cucumber Finger Sandwiches

Mini Apple Muffins

Triple Delight

Harvard Tea

Luncheon #5:

Ham and Egg Salad

Crunchy Vegetable Salad

Cherry Ribbon Salad

Herbed Bread Sticks

Cousin Pat's Peach Torte

Harvard Tea

Luncheon #6:

Tea House Chicken Salad

California Broccoli Salad

Seasonal Fruit Salad

Herbed Bread Sticks

Easy Chewy Pecan Squares

Harvard Tea

Luncheon #7:

Chicken-Fruit Salad

Creole Salad

Fresh Asparagus with Marinated Peppers

Crystallized Dill Slices

Mini Wheat Loaves

Key Lime Cake

Harvard Tea

Luncheon #8:

Sunday Brunch Casserole

Seasonal Fruit Salad

Cottage Cheese Salad with Roma Tomatoes

A+ Apricot Banana Bread

Creamy Apple Squares

Harvard Tea

Luncheon #9:

Rodeo Drive Chicken

Fifth Avenue Salad

Salad La Parisienne

Roll Ups La Costa

Millionaire Pie

Harvard Tea

Luncheon #10:

Golden Chicken Triangles

Sin-Apple Swirl Salad

Pasta Verde

Harvest Delight

Harvard Tea

Luncheon #11:

Fonduloha

Sunshine Salad

Tangy Oriental Green Bean Salad

Geri's Bread Sticks

Kapua Cake

Harvard Tea

Luncheon #12:

Garden Vegetable Pie
Vineyard Chicken Salad
Raspberry Patch Salad
Geri's Bread Sticks
Coconut Spice Cake
Harvard Tea

Luncheon #13:

Buttons & Bows Chicken Salad
Mary's Mandarin Tea Salad
Italian Marinated Vegetable Salad
Zucchini Muffins
Lemon Cheese Torte
Harvard Tea

Food for Our furry

and feathered Friends

HEARD'S MIRACLE MEAL

Woodpeckers, titmice, chickadees, cardinals, nuthatches, mockingbirds, blue jays, sparrows, wrens and bluebirds love this recipe, especially in the winter.

Place one part flour to 3 parts yellow cornmeal in large mixing bowl. Add spoonfuls of lard (not shortening) and mix with electric mixer until it makes firm balls. (Peanut butter can also be added.) Pack mixture in 1½ inch holes drilled into vertical log. Hang log by hook on one end to tree branch.

ALL SEASON SUET

- **1 cup lard (not shortening)**
- **1 cup crunchy peanut butter**
- **2 cups quick cook oats**
- **2 cups cornmeal**
- **1 cup white flour**
- **⅓ cup sugar**

Melt lard and peanut butter in large pan. Stir in remaining ingredients. Pour mixture into square freezer containers about 1½ inches thick. Allow to set up. Cut into squares to fit your feeder. Store in freezer until ready to use. This is like an ice cream treat for the birds.

Owls cannot move their eyes, but they can turn their heads so far to the right that they can actually look over their left shoulder and vice versa.

TWEET TREAT FRUIT CUPS

Keep grapefruit or orange rinds and fill with cut up apples, apricots, bananas, blueberries, cherries, cranberries, dates, grapes, peaches, pears, raisins, and/or watermelon. Secure to a tree or on platform feeder.

The feathers on an owl's wing have soft edges so it can fly more quietly in order not to be heard by its prey.

HUMMINGBIRD DELIGHT

4 parts water

1 part white granulated sugar

Boil water and add sugar until dissolved. When cool, pour into a red feeder. NEVER USE RED FOOD COLORING as it is suspected to be harmful to their kidneys. Did you know that there are 17 species of hummingbirds commonly seen in North America?

DOG GONE GOOD DOG TREATS

- **1 teaspoon instant beef bouillon**
- **½ cup hot water**
- **2¼ cups whole wheat flour**
- **1 3½-ounce jar bacon flavored pieces**
- **1 tablespoon brown sugar**
- **⅓ cup vegetable oil**
- **1 egg**

Dissolve bouillon in water. Add remaining ingredients. When well blended, roll dough out to ⅛ inch thickness. Cut out with favorite cookie cutter and put on a greased baking sheet. Bake at 300 degrees for 30-35 minutes or until firm. Store in airtight container.

Yield: 6 dozen treats

THE PURR-FECT CATNIP COOKIES

- **1 cup whole wheat flour**
- **2 tablespoons wheat germ**
- **⅓ cup soy flour**
- **⅓ cup powdered milk**
- **1 tablespoon kelp**
- **½ teaspoon bonemeal**
- **1 teaspoon crushed dried catnip leaves**
- **1 tablespoon unsulfured molasses**
- **1 egg**
- **2 tablespoons oil, butter or fat**
- **⅓ cup milk or water**

Mix the dry ingredients together. Add molasses; egg; oil, butter or fat; and milk or water. Roll out flat on an oiled cookie sheet and cut into narrow strips or ribbons. Bake at 350 degrees for 20 minutes or until lightly toasted. Break into pea-size pieces suitable for cats. Good for treats, exercising gums and cleaning teeth but too low in protein for regular food fare.

The number of eggs an owl lays depends on its supply of food.

INDEX

R

HEARD MUSEUM VOLUNTEER GUILD
One Nature Place
McKinney, Texas 75069-8840

Please send _____ copy(ies) of

Heard What's Cookin'? @ $16.95 each __________
Postage and handling @ $3.00 each __________
Texas residents add sales tax @ $1.39 each __________
TOTAL __________

Name ______________________________

Address ______________________________

City ____________________ State ______ Zip ____________

Make checks payable to ***Heard What's Cookin'?***

HEARD MUSEUM VOLUNTEER GUILD
One Nature Place
McKinney, Texas 75069-8840

Please send _____ copy(ies) of

Heard What's Cookin'? @ $16.95 each __________
Postage and handling @ $3.00 each __________
Texas residents add sales tax @ $1.39 each __________
TOTAL __________

Name ______________________________

Address ______________________________

City ____________________ State ______ Zip ____________

Make checks payable to ***Heard What's Cookin'?***

HEARD MUSEUM VOLUNTEER GUILD
One Nature Place
McKinney, Texas 75069-8840

Please send _____ copy(ies) of

Heard What's Cookin'? @ $16.95 each __________
Postage and handling @ $3.00 each __________
Texas residents add sales tax @ $1.39 each __________
TOTAL __________

Name ______________________________

Address ______________________________

City ____________________ State ______ Zip ____________

Make checks payable to ***Heard What's Cookin'?***